Girish Karnad as Playwright:

Tradition and Modernity

Girish Karnad as Playwright:
Tradition and Modernity

L.S. Gill

Prestige Books International

New Delhi

Published by

Prestige Books International

New Delhi 110 060
email: prestigebooks@gmail.com

ISBN: 978-93-82186-58-8

Printed in India

To

my wife

Kanwal Preet

and son

Anhad

who constantly inspire me to move on

Contents

Foreword

This manuscript prepared on Girish Karnad, by Dr. Lakhwinder Singh Gill and now ready for the press, attracts our attention for several reasons. One is personal for I taught him while he was doing M.A. in English literature. I was the supervisor for his Ph.D. as well. He completed his Ph.D. on the plays of this playwright. Born and brought up in a village, he did his graduation from a rural college. His alma mater for M.A. and Ph.D. was GNDU situated in Amritsar, the centre of Punjabi ethos and culture of course; he mastered English literature and is teaching the same in a postgraduate college in Amritsar. As is the vogue in postgraduate departments, the courses he teaches keep on changing. I wonder if this playwright often figures in a course comprising Indian-English literature.

These facts fail to tell why Lakhwinder Gill has resolved to bring out a full book on Girish Karnad. As already pointed out, his Ph.D. is on Girish Karnad's plays but to give a book format to his research work required further initiative. Without such an initiative and drive, how he could have decided to undertake this arduous task for someone who though belongs to a region geographically of the same country but culturally so apart from the Punjab. This is an enigma I cannot unravel in one word, phrase or even a sentence. If I do so, I can say that like Girish Karnad, he is tall, handsome, broad-shouldered, robust and elegant. But then a variation occurs that cannot be ignored. Whereas Girish Karnad's face is invariably sober, rarely showing a smile, Lakhwinder's face is ever-smiling, getting sober only on rare occasions. It was natural for so much convergence in appearance to impel him to be well-disposed to the subject of his book. Astrology and palmistry can make mountain of a molehill of a fact of this nature.

Determined to keep the molehill within its tentative limits, I am inclined to surmise that this factor might have played its part to incline Lakhwinder Gill to choose this subject. After all, friendliness is deeply ingrained in Punjabi ethos.

Apart from this tentative fact deriving from Girish Karnad's person, there is the charisma of his persona. It is a substantial factor because its range is not confined only to drama and theatre but extends to films and cinema as well. So far goes its range in drama and theatre, it is paradoxical and phenomenal at the same time. Though he has been composing his plays in his native language but it is their translation into English that has brought him widespread popularity and recognition. His situation is very much similar to that of Ibsen who was not rated high so long his plays were available only in Norwegian, his native language. It was their translation into major European languages that brought his excellence to the fore of being the first modern playwright of the western world. To rate Karnad as high as Ibsen will be a misnomer. However, he would have remained unknown to the educated Indians if his plays had not appeared in English. His *Tughlaq* was hailed as a play of iconic importance in Indian-English literature, particularly after it was staged by a very famous director. Though of a different kind, his *Naga Mandala* has also been hailed as a masterpiece in several quarters. Either of these two is likely to figure in the paper comprising Indian-English literature that began finding a place in the English literature syllabi being taught in the Indian universities and colleges. This is a substantial factor working behind Gill's resolve to publish this book.

No doubt, Girish Karnad's persona has worked wonders for bringing him fame and recognition, which go across national boundaries and seek habitation and name in other English-speaking countries. Has his persona remained commensurate with his person, is a rather ticklish issue that needs to be pondered over a bit in this context. It is not out of place to hold that inconsistency between the two has prevailed from the beginning. Whereas consistency between the two brings him social prestige, it may not enhance his creativity as inconsistency is likely to do provided it does not end up as discordance. That of late this inconsistency tends to turn into discordance cannot be denied. For example, he played central role as Praneshacharya in the film based on Ananthamurthy's celebrated novel *Samskara*. This role, that he played about five decades back, brought him great glory and ushered his career first in the regional and then the Hindi films. He professed deep friendship with the novelist Ananthamurthy, which the latter also reciprocated in equal measure. But this friendship lacked friendliness and it is this lack that has led him to term this celebrated novel as shallow and meaningless. These comments he has made after the novelist is no longer in this world to take cognizance of them. Sometime back, he spoke against Rabindranath Tagore whom he had revered. Both the incidents beget the impression that unresolved tension always remains in his mind vis-à-vis his person and persona. If earlier, it was latent, of late it has got manifest. When it was latent, the sources, history, legend and myth providing him the resources, would come under its signature. Most of all, his language faced odds while getting apportioned to the different characters. Though it may sound hazardous to contend, but I dare do so that in forging dramatic language, he has lagged behind in devising incidents and organizing them into plots.

This study does not include *The Dreams of Tipu Sultan*. Maybe this play of Karnad fails to rise to the level from which he has not generally slipped. Why he did not think it proper to impart present meaning to past significance as he was so successful in doing in *Tughlaq* is an issue that deserves to be debated at several levels of unresolved problematic between his person and persona. This is not the proper forum for this debate. As the new dispensation, overtly arousing his antipathy but covertly doing the opposite, comes fully in the open, this debate will become not only indispensable but inevitable as well.

Lakhwinder Gill has remained discreet while charting themes, relations, tensions in his plays. For evidences he has looked very closely. The variations, occurring in them, rarely miss his minute observation. This goes a long way not only in unraveling the individual plays but also in relating them. His whole effort, no doubt admirable, presents Girish Karnad's all plays as integral parts of his oeuvre. A perspective comes to the fore, which could have extended in scope through the correlation of his achievement in the domain of film and cinema. But it might have harmed the trajectory of which this book shows them as integral components.

Interestingly, Lakhwinder has concluded by looking at his subject in comparative projection. He has compared and contrasted Karnad's first play *Yayati* with *Fate* by Sant Singh Sekhon, a renowned Punjabi playwright. Both the plays draw their material from tradition and put them in the light of modern sensibility. Sekhon's *Fate* seems to score over Girish Karnad's earliest play for exploring psychological conflict surging between youth and age, love and passion, duty and obligation enriching our understanding about Karnad as well. Perhaps Girish Karnad, himself, will not miss to go through this chapter.

Tejwant Singh Gill

Author's Note

A village boy becoming a Rhodes Scholar in England, a student of Mathematics and Statistics writing plays and translating those plays into English and winning Jnanpith Award the highest literary honour in India- are some paradoxical facts about Girish Karnad that have always fascinated me. The way his rural background has worked as a strength rather than hurdle is rather enthusing.

I take it as a matter of pride to have done Ph.D on Girish Karnad and now to bring out my second book on the writer. After completing my Ph.D. when I wrote him a letter, he was gracious enough to reply: "I need scarcely say how touched I am that you devoted so much of your energy, time and labour for the study of my works. What else can an author ask for?" These lines have always been a source of joy and satisfaction for me.

I feel obliged to Dr. Tejwant Singh Gill, a renowned scholar and critic of English and Punjabi literature, who motivated me to pursue research on Girish Karnad. Without his guidance, the present book could not be a reality.

I am also grateful to Dr. R.K. Dhawan, Professor, University of Delhi, for being so supportive and positive whenever I called upon him.

My gratitude is due to the Sahitya Akademi, New Delhi, for publishing my article 'Two Indian Plays: Oedipus Complex in Counterpoint' in its prestigious journal *Indian Literature* (Volume 223). The same article is reproduced here in the final chapter as 'A Comparative Projection' for better understanding of Girish Karnad.

Lakhwinder Singh Gill

Girish Karnad and Indian English Drama: Introduction

Girish Karnad is not only an extremely innovative modern Indian playwright of the post-independence India but also an acclaimed actor and director of theatre and films. He is one of the modern playwrights like Vijay Tendulkar, Badal Sircar and Mahesh Dattani who have given a new direction to Indian English drama. But unlike his contemporaries he is constantly engaged in deconstructing mythical and historical incidents with a view to giving them a current meaning. As a modern playwright he takes up mythical and legendary tales from his own culture and unfolds them in the light of modern sensibility. This art of deconstructing myths becomes an act of self-searching for the playwright. In his hands, common folk tales assume contemporary significance. Because of his fondness for juxtaposing the past and the present, it is essential to have a look at Karnad's background as a playwright.

Born in 1938, Girish Karnad grew up in a small town Sirsi, Karnataka, which lacked even the basic facilities like electricity. The only source of entertainment was the tales about regional myths and legends that had characters from the supernatural world. Mythical stories heard from elders were almost a part of living for the people of Sirsi. Spending childhood in a village also provided Karnad an opportunity to have first-hand experience with the folk theatre in Karnataka. The folk tales narrated by his grandmother and presented on the stage by the Natak companies, which toured his native place occasionally, left a permanent mark on his mind that later formed the basis of Karnad's vision as a playwright. His childhood experience of *Yakshagana* in Sirsi, his experience of urban theatre in Bombay where he went for his postgraduate studies, influenced the artist in Karnad. On an evening when he was watching Strindberg's *Miss Julie* directed by Ebrahim Alkazi, the playwright in him suddenly woke up. In the introduction to *Three Plays: Nagamandala, Hayavadana and Tughlaq*, he narrates this unique experience thus:

> I had read some western playwrights in college but nothing had prepared me for the power and violence I experienced that day. By the norms I had brought up on, the very notion of laying bare the inner recesses of the human psyche like this for public consumption seemed obscene. What impressed me as much as the psychological cannibalism of the play was the way lights faded in and out on stage . . . the realization that there were instruments called Dimmers that could gently fade the lights in or out opened up a whole new world of magical possibilities. . . . I have often wondered whether it was not that evening that without being actually aware of it I decided I wanted to be a playwright.

So it was in 1961 that the man, who initially wanted to be a poet, then a novelist, became a playwright with his first play *Yayati*.

Karnad's upbringing of the rural type always haunts him as an artist. He always tends to combine his past and present into a unity that bespeaks of tradition and modernity in his art of playwriting. In order to understand him as a playwright it is essential to understand the concept of tradition and modernity.

According to *Encyclopedia of Religion*, "A belief of practice may be said to be tradition to the extent that it is received from hands, lips or from the example of others rather than being discovered or invented."So 'discovery' or 'invention' is not the feature of the belief that forms tradition. Instead of being invented, a belief is passed on to generations without losing touch with its origin: it is transmitted from one person to another and from generation to generation without any substantial change. So, on one hand, tradition is essentially related to the past and, on the other, it implies movement or action through time.

Derived from the word 'modern,' modernity has only time significance. 'Modern' simply means an idea, a thing or a person belonging to the recent times. Today's modern will not be so after some passage of time. For being modern essential is the departure from the exemplary model of the past, "a decentring of habitual ways of viewing the world, the necessity for producing normative standards out of one self. This is combined with an opening to the future."[2] The notion of the modern undergoes semantic shift much faster than similar terms of comparable function like romantic or neo-classical. It is also distinguished from antique, ancient or medieval. Modernity goes with years: it explicitly identifies openness and a commitment to the new as opposed to the old.

Modernity must be distinguished in meaning from other related terms like modernism and contemporaneity. To quote Niharranjan Ray: "Modernism is a term which was, to begin with, understood in a theological context: It connoted in the main, subordination of creeds, dogmas and scriptural authority to analysis and criticism, textual, historical or otherwise, in the light of science and reason. It is thus qualitative in significance and hence a value."[4] It is simply a quality of being modern—it has come to connote forms, ideas, visions, modes, or methods characteristic of present or recent times, which ultimately in terms of art and theatre connotes qualities of thought, expression, form and style which are the features of present times. The writer or the artist who accepts these qualities is a modernist. Thus the term modernity has relative significance. It seeks to explain the values of the present in terms of the past. This concept is bound by temporal and spatial considerations. However, it is not to be confused with contemporaneity. If modernity is a comparative concept, contemporaneity has absolute significance. Modernity is viewed with implicit reference to the past and the word contemporary definitely connoted awareness or full consciousness and understanding of our times.

Before we discuss 'tradition' with reference to Karnad's plays we must get an idea of Indian English drama in the background of which Karnad's plays are to be discussed. In fact, Indian English drama has no rich history of its own. It was in 1871 that Michael Madhusudan Datt wrote his first English play titled *Is This the Civilization?* Thereafter, no substantial effort was made for decades together. "Among the various forms of Indian writing in English, drama seems to lag far behind poetry and fiction."[5] First of all, drama being a composite art which needs various accessories such as actors, audience and stage could not appropriate them adequately enough in India. Second, English being a foreign language proved rather a big hindrance for the growth of Indian drama. Neither the English playwrights could express themselves so consummately, nor could the actors act in a natural way. Moreover, English was not intelligible to the masses. They could not comprehend the intricacies of the foreign language. For these reasons English drama in India suffered a lot and the Indian theatre has been defined only by playwriting in the regional languages.

Indian English drama made its humble beginning in the 19th century Bengal. Noteworthy contribution was of Rabindranath Tagore, Sri Aurobindo, T.P. Kailasam, A.P.S. Ayyar, Harindranath Chattopadhyaya and Bharati Sarabhai. Gradually, the hang-up of English as a foreign language began losing ground and more Indian English playwrights appeared on the scene. Asif Currimbhoy, P.A. Krishnaswami, and Sardar Joshi are the other important playwrights of the era of the post-Independence.

Indian English theatre, which Girish Karnad inherited, too, does not have a long history. It made its humble beginning with the British support in the second half of the 19th century. The three major Indian cities—Bombay, Madras and Calcutta—the important trade centres under the influence of British trading companies, became the centre of the theatre activity. Till late, the Indian English drama could not make substantial progress and grew only in the shadow of the British theatre. After independence, the impetus imparted to theatrical activity in India took various forms like the establishment of National School of drama. But this also helped the growth of theatre in regional languages. Barring a few occasional performances in the big cities, there is almost no living English theatre in India.

If we take into account some modern playwrights like Vijay Tendulkar and Mahesh Dattani they seem to have demolished the traditional pattern of Indian drama and established their own. Vijay Tendulkar with his *Sakharam Binder* and *Silence! The Court is in Session* interrogates the sexual moral standards of the middle class Indian society. In *Ghashiram Kotwal* he exposes the power politics of marginalization and subjugation on the basis of caste, class and gender. The theme of violence dominates his thinking as a playwright. Mahesh Dattani, on the other hand, brings into light the issues that remain unexplored by other playwrights. He picks up those sensational issues of our society which remained untouchable so far. In his plays like Se*ven Steps around the Fire*, *On a Muggy Night in Mumbai*, *Do the Needful*, *Final Solutions, Dance like a Man,* and *Bravely Fought the Queen* he dares to expose the life of gays, lesbians and *hijras*.

One of the reasons which are responsible for meagre achievement of Indian English drama is the playwrights' failure to employ rich folk forms and traditional models and techniques of the classical Sanskrit drama. Looking to the west for plots, themes and techniques does not help at all. Sometimes the love for theatre and playwriting gets confined to translations of English plays only. A few playwrights have taken advantage of the traditional Indian theatre and attempted new interpretations of Indian myths and legends: Girish Karnad is such a playwright. Basically tradition for him is only a corpus of myths, legends and sometimes historically true events. Instead of depending upon on the west for his themes and techniques, he experiments with the traditional tales and techniques. As a result, he remains close to tradition as regards his style and content.

The influences working on Girish Karnad's art are varied in nature. Apart from Dr. Bendre and K. Kurtkoti, the theatre personalities of Karnataka, the European modernists like Camus and Sartre have exercised considerable impact on Girish Karnad.[5] Besides, his first-hand experiences with the western culture and roots in the mythological past marks his plays with a distinctive mood of tension and dilemma. This is further strengthened by the joys and challenges of independent India that saw not only the end of the colonial empire but also the beginning of a new nation. The joy of freedom brought with it new fears and challenges. If this phase was a departure from the past, it was also in continuity with the old. The subjects and the institutions remained the same but the indigenous rulers were different. Soon the joy of independence began to give place to disillusionment. The dreams of justice, equality and prosperity began to wither away and new problems as of communalism, corruption and selfishness cropped up. On the world scene too, the influence of Karl Marx, Lenin and Sigmund Freud's thought on one hand, and, of Eliot, Joyce and Ezra Pound on the other made their dent. No twentieth century writer could shut his eyes to such formidable influences. The economic, political, psychological and scientific developments on the national and international scene drove Karnad into a dilemma. That is why he always contemplates over the mythological past, encountered with reference to the present.

The next major influence that haunts him always is his parental background of the rural type. The traditional up-bringing provided him with the opportunity to have first-hand experience with the folk theatre in Karnataka. Living in a joint family and listening to the folk tales and then viewing these tales being staged, rooted Girish Karnad deep in his tradition. Asked what are the reasons for not breaking away from his past and setting his own agenda, he replies:

> I think one reason is because I grew up in Sirsi. At that time, there was no electricity. I stayed in Sirsi from 1941 to 1952. That means the day used to get over by 8 o'clock in the evening. There was no television, and I grew up by lantern light. The whole atmosphere was of stories. There was one lady who would cook for us. She used to stay with us and tell stories at dusk. In school, we used to tell stories to each other. One of the reasons I can write about mythical characters so easily is because they were a part of my growing up.[6]

The folk tales heard in the light of a lantern formed the basis of his vision as a playwright. In this context a critic remarks, "The rich wealth of folklore, told and retold amidst the frightening darkness of the surrounding jungles transported the little boy to a world where snake spoke like a man and Gods changed form."

The practice of going back to mythology is not totally new in Indian English drama. The playwrights even before Girish Karnad, have drawn stories from mythology and interpreted them anew. S. Krishna Bhatta observes, "Some people right from Michael Madhusudan Dutt's *Sharmishtha* (1859) unto Girish Karnad's *Yayati* (1961) and the *Hayavadana* (1975) illustrate the growth of the playwrights' desire to give a modern interpretation to mythology." Karnad too realizes that the relationship between theatre and mythology is very close. As the function of theatre is to reflect society which is best signified in myths, the best reservoir of myths is the epics which are "the repositories of the ethnic memory. They are taken out of archetypal myths and become a part of the collective unconscious of the people. So they reflect the ethos and the psyche of a group of people, not only in a given temporal frame but have a universal human context." It is thus impossible for a writer like Karnad to depict reality of human experience without drawing upon the epics.

The division we generally make of time into present, past and future exists only on the conscious level. At the subconscious or unconscious level there is no such compartmentalization. That is why myths being the representatives of our subconscious and unconscious mind never get old. In the Indian context, the *Upanishads*, the *Ramayana*, the *Mahabharata* and the popular *Puranas* like the *Bhagvata* have entered into the very fabric of the Indian society. We find our culture best portrayed in them. The author of the great Hindu epic, *The Mahabharata*, genuinely says with pride 'that which cannot be found here exists nowhere.' Moreover, there is a technical advantage for a writer to draw his material from mythology, i.e., it gives him veiled freedom to comment upon the subtle issues which otherwise, because of their religious and social sensitivity, are difficult to tackle. During the British days when direct critique was not possible, historical or mythical stories were employed by the playwrights as a cover to give the message of revolt to the Indians against the Britishers. In this project Girish Karnad does not stand alone. But what makes him different from others is the fact that unlike his predecessors or contemporaries, his concern with the past is more psychological than social or religious or political. In the old stories, he finds the depiction of man's behaviour with all its intricacies. The mythological and the historical characters have strong affinity with modern experience as regards its psychological and emotional dilemmas. Karnad makes myths and legends a vehicle of a new vision as he tries to show the absurdity of life with all its elemental passion and conflicts and man's eternal struggle to achieve perfection.

The playwright's immense interest in mythological past is also due to the fact that myths remain an integral part of the living culture in India. The deities of the Indian pantheon are a part and parcel of the day-to-day life of the people. Because of their long association with the deities, the supernatural world is more a fact than fiction for Indians. Hence, living in an age of reason and science, Karnad doesn't lose touch with tradition, mythology and history which remain a repository of ideas for him.

In an interview published in *The Hindu*, Karnad reveals how by using myths he gets the liberty of "flirting with ideas":

> Maybe I cannot invent plots. I go in for stories that are exciting; I think these are better stories than I will be able to botch up. At least in this want of originality, I am perhaps as good, or as bad, as Shakespeare. . . . One thing more, I turn out only to myths legends and history, but also to folklore. In fact, what attracts me most is the archetypal folk tale; with no fact already there. I find in it all the scope for flirting with ideas. I find the great advantage of being able to subvert the traditional, even classical beliefs. Since folk tales make fun of everybody—rulers, priests, even gods—everything is taken in good humour.

This response of Girish Karnad is not only a compliment on the rich and the unexplored culture he belongs to, but also a hint at his artistic ability with which he can shape and reshape the old material.

NOTES

1. Ernest Behlar, "Modernism and Postmodernism in Contemporary Thought," *Irony and the Discourse of Modernity* (United States of America: University of Washington Press, 1936), p. 3.
2. Girish Karnad, An Interview with Kirtinath Kurtkoti, *Contemporary Indian Theatre: Interviews with Playwrights and Directors* (New Delhi, Sangeet Natak Akademi, 1989), p. 79.
3. Malcolm Bradbury and James McFarlane, "The Name and Nature of Modernism," *Modernism* (Norwich: University of East Angolia, 1974), p.22
4. Niharranjan Ray, "Inaugural Address," *Modernity and Contemporary Indian Literature: Proceedings of a Seminar* (Shimla: Indian Institute of Advanced Study, 1968), p. 4.
5. *Ibid.*, p. 4.
6. S. Krishna Bhatta, *Indian English Drama: A Critical Study* (New Delhi: Sterling, 1987), p. 1.
7. Samskrati S. Gulvadi, "Playing with the Past" (Interview), *The Deccan Herald*, 8 August 1992.

Tradition and Modernity

Tradition in Girish Karnad is constituted by myths, legends and mythical tales which travel from generation to generation as carriers of human feelings. Girish Karnad picks them up to introduce changes as per his dramatic requirements. He narrates them in such a way that they tend to mirror present reality. Interestingly, these folk tales become the tales of the modern man living under the impact of current western ideologies. Thus, tradition and modernity intertwine with each other in order to focus on the present reality. As a playwright Girish Karnad is rooted in Indian tradition and as a man of late 20th century his thought grows up in the shadow of the contemporary philosophies. About his concern for tradition and modernity, Veena Noble Dass says, "He has been in the west and has been attracted by the drama of the Giraudoux, Albert Camus and Jean-Paul Sartre in his search for new forms of drama. . . . His reworking of myths Puranic, historical and literary, relates him to Kailasam and Rangacharya as much as it does to those European dramatists who remake their myths."

For Girish Karnad the best source of tradition is the *Mahabharata*, the *Puranas* and the historically true incidents that, he believes, are still contextual for the modern times. He draws correspondences between the past and the present, from myth and history to real life to depict current psychological problems. In fact he revisited myths and legends and made them a vehicle of new ideas. His first play *Yayati* and the later plays *Hayavadana* and *The Fire and the Rain* are based on the *Puranic* stories whereas *Nagamandala* draws material from a very common oral tale. The other source for Karnad is the regional and national historical events and his *Tughlaq* and *Tale-Danda* are examples of their transmutation. However, he does not accept the traditional stories as sacrosanct at all: he picks up only the useful part of it and makes arbitrary changes.

His first play *Yayati* dramatizes a story from the *Mahabharata.* It is not unusual for Karnad to make changes to the myth to suit his convenience. Yayati's story is thus no exception. The mythical story goes that the king Nahusha had six sons and Yayati was one of them. Devyani, who unsuccessfully loved Kacha later, married Yayati. She nursed a strong feeling of hatred for Sharmishtha with whom she had close association during childhood days. Sharmishtha loved Yayati and underwent great physical and mental torture for love; a son Puru was born to them. Yayati in his craze for sensuous joys dreaded old age. Puru, Sharmishtha's son, offered to exchange his youth for the old age of his father. The enlightened Yayati gave up his crown and retired to forest life to lead a life of renunciation with Devyani and Sharmishtha. Girish Karnad introduces a few dramatic changes in this story but retains Yayati's love for life and his final renunciation. In the *Mahabharata*, Yayati recognizes the nature of desire itself and realizes that fulfillment does not diminish or finish desire. In Karnad's play, however, Yayati recognizes the horror of his own life and assumes his moral responsibility after a series of symbolic encounters.

The plot is built up against the backdrop of rigid caste lines and a few supernatural elements: two inherent features of Indian tradition. The origin of *Yayati* and its relevance with the present is hinted at when Sutradhar says: "it is a Puranic play—a page from the history unknown past . . . though it is a story of our ancestors, we find our own image in it."[1] Devyani and Sharmishtha are childhood friends. They love each other very much and feel they cannot live without each other. But one day when they are bathing in a river and Sharmishtha puts on Devyani's 'kanchaki,' the latter's inner caste-ridden self jumps out. She starts abusing her.

She reminds Sharmishtha of her low birth and warns her not to forget her social origin. Shocked and humiliated, Sharmishtha pushes Devyani into a well nearby. When she cries aloud helplessly from inside the well her cries are heard by the king Yayati who incidentally is passing by. He pulls her out and recognizes her as the daughter of Shukracharya who has *Sanjeevani* (a herb) enabling a person to stay young for ever. Ambitious to have permanent youth, Yayati marries her and Sharmishtha becomes his attendant. One day when Devyani is away and Sharmishtha is alone with Yayati, he seduces her. On learning of this relationship, Devyani gets furious. Cursing Sharmishtha and her husband she leaves for her father's place who curses Yayati for deceiving his daughter. Due to the curse Yayati turns old but there is a concession, i.e., the curse of old age can be shifted to someone else who may own the responsibility of king's guilt. Feeling helpless before the nature of curse, the king begs everybody to relieve him of it. But none else than his own son Puru comes forward to help him at this juncture. As a result, the curse of the old age gets shifted from Yayati to Puru—from the father to the son. But Yayati fails to stand the challenges of new life. His failure to do so leads to his final renunciation for a forest life of complete isolation. Thus, the liaison between Yayati and Devyani and the birth of Puru remains the major dramatic deviation from the original myth.

Karnad's *The Fire and the Rain* provides another illustration. In the preface the playwright comments upon the origin of the plot saying, "The myth of Yavakri (or Yavakrita) occurs in chapter 135-138 of the *Vana Purva* (Forest Canto) of the *Mahabharata*. It is narrated by the ascetic Lomasha to the Pandavas as they wander across the land during their exile."[2] Thus the play emerges from a minor myth in the *Mahabharata*.

The action of the play involves two brothers—Paravasu and Arvasu. Paravasu is the chief priest of the fire sacrifice being conducted by the king to propitiate Indra, and Arvasu is an inspiring actor. The other main character is Yavakri who in order to take revenge of his father's humiliation caused by his uncle Raibhya undertakes penance. He gets the 'knowledge' of the Vedas direct from the gods rather than from any human being. Finally, his wish is granted by Indra. Yavakri, who has always nourished a feeling of vengeance against Raibhya, becomes able to wreak it on him by seducing Vishakha, his daughter-in-law, on the pretence of his love for her. Knowing that Yavakri has deceived her and is bent upon meeting the Brahmin-Rakshasa sent by her father-in-law, Vishakha pours out his life-saving water. The horrified Yavakri runs towards his father's hermitage where he could hide himself. But the blind man who guards the hermitage bars Yavakri's entry and he is killed by the Rakshasa. On the other hand, Raibhya gets killed by his own son Paravasu. Instead of taking the responsibility of his father's murder, he holds his younger brother Arvasu responsible for it. Finally, it is only with the intervention of Arvasu that the god of rain is pleased and it rains to the relief of everyone. About the traditional origin of the play, Girish Karnad in his interview with Ratnottama Sengupta says: "The basic metaphor in the play is of a 'Yajna,' the first sacrifice, for the sake of rain. The complicated plot is one of the subsidiary stories of the *Mahabharata*. It does not have the main characters. It devolves upon Lomoshatya—one of the Rishis the Pandavas came upon during the vanavasa. . . . It is probably my most complex to date. What interest me were these norms of Hindu religion like *tapas*, doing penance or the fire sacrifice to please the gods."

As in the basic myth of Yayati, Karnad brings in some changes in this myth also. Paravasu and Yavakri are not the sons of two close friends but of two real brothers. The plot becomes the revenge story of a family having close resemblance with the story of Kauravas and Pandavas in the *Mahabharata*. The education of Vishakha by Yavakri may be an individual stroke of the playwright but it looks acceptable as Vishakha's husband has been staying away from her for seven years. As a chief priest leaving the sacrifice incomplete, he cannot visit his wife back home. On the other hand, Vishakha's fury to deprive Yavakri of his life-saving water is a convincing incident after she finds out that she is made only an instrument by him to satiate his feelings of vengeance. The reference to their mutual past is also a joyous relief for the audience. Then the creation of a simple-minded fun-loving hunter girl and her innocent and joyous exchanges of love with Arvasu are a welcome relief in the otherwise tense atmosphere of the play.

The plot of *Hayavadana* comes from *Kathasaritsagara*—a collection of stories in Sanskrit. The dramatist borrows it through Thomas Mann's retelling of the story in his *Transposed Heads*. Mann ridicules the basic concept of differentiating between the body and the soul. But Karnad employs the mythical story with a different purpose. The play which starts with the worship of Ganesha, employs a mythical tale presenting three human characters: Devadatta, Kapila and a beautiful girl Padmini apart from a semi-human figure Hayavadana—who has the body of a human being and the head of a horse. Devadatta is a scholar with frail body and Kapila is a wrestler with very attractive physique. They are good friends loving each other a lot. In fact, the people compare them with Rama and Lakshmana. Devadatta falls in love with Padmini and Kapila, being his fast friend, helps Devadatta in marrying her. After they get married, Devadatta grows suspicious about the mutual attraction between Kapila and his wife who always cherishes the beautiful muscular body of Kapila which Devadatta lacks. One day when the three are at Rudra's temple, Kapila and Padmini go for excursion leaving Devadatta behind. He fails to stand the pain caused by this association between his close friend and his wife. Unable to wait any more he goes to the temple of the Goddess Kali and cuts his head off in frustration. When Kapila and Padmini come back, they find him missing. Kapila later finds him in the temple of Kali with his head cut off.

Scared of what the people would think of their friendship he too beheads himself. Padmini also reaches the site and to her utter confusion finds both her husband and his friend dead. She starts blaming the goddess Kali for being present and doing nothing to avert the tragedy. So she prays to the goddess to help her. Moved by her prayer the goddess grants her permission to bring back the dead to life by joining the respective heads over their bodies. What complicates her problem is that she joins Devadatta's head over Kapila's body and vice-versa. But it further complicates her problem. She resolves to stay with the body that has Devadatta's head as according to the *Shastras* head represents the body. The new combination, however, fails to please her for long. One day, she goes back to Kapila who lives in a forest. Her reunion with Kapila too does not last long as Devadatta joins them soon. At the end, all the three characters meet their destined end. The playwright's invention of Hayavadana, the semi-human figure, and some other incidents contribute to the development of the play.

Nagamandala is another experiment from the angle of tradition and modernity. It revolves around a female character Rani who is married to a cruel and inhuman husband Appanna. From the very first day of his marriage Appanna treats her as a slave. Mostly he stays out with his concubine and visits his wife only for meals. In her effort to win back her callous husband, Rani, with the help of Kurudavva, gets attracted towards the king cobra, living in a mole hill of her courtyard. The root that Kurudavva gives her for her husband to take is eaten by the cobra. Thereafter, it starts visiting her bed-room in the form of her husband which leads to Rani's conception. When it comes to the knowledge of Appanna he turns furious as he has never shared bed with Rani. To prove her promiscuity, he brings it to the knowledge of the Village-Elders. But this ordeal turns in her favour and she becomes a goddess for the villagers and for her husband too. He accepts her as his sincere and ideal wife and they begin to lead a perfectly harmonious life. The cobra is given a permanent place in Rani's hair and it becomes a part of her body forever. Thus an oral tale assumes multi-dimensional meanings in the hands of the playwright.

Wrestling with tradition and modernity through historical material is Karnad's forte in *Tughlaq* and *Tale-Danda. Tughlaq* is the story of the monarch who came to the throne by murdering his father and brother and ruled over India for about 20 years. He is wise and foolish, kind and cruel, impulsive and farsighted in one breath. His two major decisions—the shifting of his capital from Delhi to Daulatabad and the change in currency—backfire. Instead of benefitting his subjects they render them homeless. Muhammad trying to be a just king turns out to be unjust at times. He kills many of his associates including his stepmother because he doubts their sincerity towards him. He wants to do everything possible for the welfare of his people. But neither does the king understand his subjects, nor do the subjects understand him as a ruler. This gap leads to the total chaos in the state, leaving Muhammad a broken man at the end. The vigour and determination he has in the beginning is lost at the end. The prayer-scene and the characters like Aziz, Aazam and the stepmother, however, are dramatic inventions of the playwright to match the purpose.

If *Tughlaq* draws its material from the Indian history, Karnad's *Tale-Danda* derives it from a regional incident in the history of Karnataka that took place in the city of Kalyan in the 12th century. Eight hundred years ago, in the city of Kalyan, a man called Basavanna assembled a congregation of poets, mystics, social revolutionaries and philosophers. They were unmatched for their creativity and social commitment in the history of Karnataka. They opposed idolatry, rejected temple worship and upheld the equality of sexes and rejected discrimination between human beings on the basis of caste and creed. Events took a violent turn when they brought their belief of casteless society into practice. The movement that was started for a social cause ended in bloodshed. A prosperous society plunged into anarchy and terror. *Tale-Danda*[3] picturizes only one week of those turbulent days. In the play, the movement for the social justice is carried by Basavanna who is also King Bijjala's treasurer, and by Jagadeva who is the son of an orthodox Brahmin family. Crossing all the barriers of caste and creed they and their followers call themselves the Sharanas. The king Bijjala suppresses this movement ruthlessly. Though he himself is a Shudra, the policy of Sharanas does not suit him. He does not appreciate the idea of inter-caste marriage between a Brahmin girl and a low-caste boy. Despite his policy of avoiding moral responsibility as a king, he is finally killed by the Sharanas. The movement which initially aims to eradicate social evils ends in disaster as the Sharanas too get scattered at the end.

Modernity in Karnad's Plays

Karnad's fondness for tradition does not mean propagating any religious or spiritual thought. His interest is in the modern man and his psychological problems. By employing these myths he tries to show the absurdity of life with all its elemental passions and conflicts and man's eternal struggle to achieve perfection. In this way, Karnad presents reality through old stories: he reflects the present through the past. His outlook towards the present is coloured by the prevalent philosophies like Darwinism, Marxism, Freudism, and Existentialism.

Darwin's ideas of the origin, differentiation and evolution of the species outrightly rejecting ideas of man's metaphysical origin place him in a world where survival belongs to the strong, the ruthless and the biologically lucky but not to the moral or the just. Then the Marxian ideology also wrought a fundamental change in man-to-man relationship holding that economic factor is the essential determinant in human relationships. According to Marxism there are only 'haves' and 'have-nots' and human society can be divided into these two classes only. There is a natural clash of interests between the two: one being the 'exploiter' and the other the 'exploited.' The Marxian interpretation of society forwards the concepts of liberty, freedom and equality. Equipped with them, man is disposed to question the moral and religious values which hold that everything is predetermined and beyond human initiative and will. Freudism, too, by exploring the human mind emphasizes the unconscious drives and libidinal forces as determining behaviour. He explains human relationships on the basis of sexual urge and views religion and morality as a part of social mechanism aimed to have a check on man's natural self which, if given free hand, can destabilize human civilization. Existentialism is also a reaction against rationalism and traditional systems that have been valuing reason and imposing social norms and standards upon man. In the light of all this, Karnad deconstructs myths and questions old system of values. As he himself says, "The energy of folk theatre comes from the fact that although it seems to uphold traditional values, it also has the means of questioning these values and making them literally stand on their head."[4] This is true to his plays.

It is under the impact of the modern theories like Freudism that a sort of Oedipus complex appears to mark all mother-son relationships in the traditional plots of Girish Karnad. Oedipus, a prominent figure in Greek mythology, killed his father and married his mother. As such, in Freud's Oedipus complex, the son has incestuous attachment with his mother and a feeling of jealousy and hatred for his father. There is an unconscious feeling in him to take his father's position and be the unperturbed recipient of his mother's love.

Prior to the emergence of the Phallic period, a boy loves his mother and identifies himself with his father; when the sexual urge increases the boy's love for his mother becomes incestuous and as a result he becomes jealous of his rival, the father. This state of affairs in which the boy causes exclusive sexual possession of the mother and feels antagonistic towards the father is called the Oedipus complex.[5]

The development of this oedipal feeling also creates a new danger for the boy, i.e., he can be physically harmed by his father. This fear in the unconscious mind leads to boy's hatred for his father

Freudianism

In *Yayati* Puru's obsession with his mother and his willingness to accept his father's old age may be viewed from the Freudian angle. When Puru is away from his mother he can not forget her. He confesses that his mother's memory always haunts him: he misses even the room where he used to be with his mother, "my dear room! . . . the room of a few moments of enjoyment in life!" About his mother he always dreams who she was and what she was like. Even when alone, he doesn't think of anything except the room they would share. In every possible way he hints at his attraction for his mother but his father fails to understand him. Puru holds that Yayati never had time to ask him the question about his inner self. To have answers to such questions "he was always restless." This also shows that his existence for him is only in relation to his mother. His decision to accept the old age of his father is an attempt in this direction to satisfy the desires of his sub-conscious mind. He always questions his father about "that one face" only. At last, when his father does not give him satisfactory reply, he cries. His hatred for Yayati is also not a secret. To Freud, the father is always an obstacle for the son between him and his mother. His hatred for the father never dies. Yayati too makes confession of this hostile relationship when he admits that whenever they talk to each other there is a quarrel and Puru "vomits fire" seeing him.

Karnad carries on the Freudian motives and the idea of Oedipus complex further in *Tughlaq*. Muhammad has killed his father and is very much attached to his stepmother. She too feels much concerned over his not being married yet. She feels worried about his late nights and asks: "Then what do you do all night" (155). She just wants to know why he never seems to go to his "bed" at all. At this Muhammad shouts: "Don't tell me to go and get married and breed a family because I won't sleep." Bursting into laughter she says, "I don't know what to do with you." Later, when she finds out that Najib is too close to Muhammad and is in full possession of him, she feels jealous. She goes to the extent of murdering him. When Muhammad comes to know of it, his attachment to his mother turns into wrath.

Freud also holds that too much attachment between the mother and the son results only in unusual jealousy and anger:

> A boy has not merely an ambivalent attitude towards his father and an affectionate relationship with his mother but at the same time he also behaves like a girl and displays an affectionate feminine attitude to his father and corresponding hostility and jealousy towards his mother.[6]

This is what impels Muhammad to call her adulterous. His sexual aggression comes to the fore and he shouts "woman, woman, so you are also one of them! So that's what you too wanted! . . . And now you too are trying the same game, aren't you? Get rid of Najib, so that you could control me" (204). And "Clever you. You thought I won't punish you, didn't you? Because I love you more than I have loved anyone in my life." Calling her worse than an adulterous he wants her stoned to death publicly to show to the people "how an adulterous dies."

In *Tale-Danda* too, the father-son relationship is in no way cordial. They do not tolerate each other. Sovideva does not have respect for Bijjala nor does Bijjala have high opinion about his son. Significantly, they hold Rambha responsible for the bitterness between them. On learning that in his absence Sovideva tried to temper with the treasury records, he at once starts abusing and cursing him. He thinks that his wife has pampered him with her love: "Rambha! Rambha! All this is your loving. You, with your rampaging and swaddling, have turned him into a royal eunuch" (11). Because of his disliking for him, he wants to have "birched the skin off his back and to have tied him up in a bundle and downed him in a river." But she always stood "in the middle," feels he. Rambha also holds that Bijjala treats her son as one shouldn't treat even one's bitterest enemy. When Sovideva stands answerless before him, Bijjala's reaction has sexual connotations. He remarks that he cannot use his tongue but is quick enough "to find the wrong limb to do the wrong things."

From the angle of mutual bond between Rambhavati and Sovideva it is important that Sovideva has not been able to keep his marriage intact. When his mother finds him roaming around, she symbolically suggests to her husband about Sovideva's marriage: "He has come of age and you haven't even thrown a scrap of land at him" (12). 'Land' in the Freudian sense means 'womb.' When fearing his father Sovideva hides himself with his mother, Bijjala calls out, "come out, come out, aren't you ashamed to hide between a woman's legs, you blood-sodden rag. You—what were you upto in my absence?" When he starts beating him, Rambhavati comes to Sovideva's defence as the relationship between the mother and the son is very powerful: "I beg you, don't. Don't beat him, please. . . . I beg you. He's a grown-up man." Later, when Sovideva wearing his father's crown is seen by his mother, she asks him to take off the crown. But Sovideva remains unmoved. At this, the king's remarks are very symbolic: "So! perhaps you do have something between your legs after all." When Sovideva refuses to take off the crown, his mother remarks, "curse be on your head." It reminds us of Oedipus Rex who under a curse seduced his own mother.

The Oedipal connotation in *The Fire and the Rain* may not be so strong but the relationship between Paravasu and his father Raibhya is definitely antagonistic. When Paravasu clandestinely crawls out of the sacrifice premises for meeting his wife in the middle of night, Raibhya scolds him for doing what he was not expected to do, being the chief priest. His behaviour smacks of abhorrence for Paravasu. He taunts him saying, "I told the king . . . my son defecates wherever he goes and he will defecate in your presence" (29). When the king called him younger and more fit to be the chief priest Raibhya felt "aggrieved." He was sure that "he will outlive his sons." He does not compromise with the situation. Later, he seems to settle scores with Paravasu by torturing his wife when she has to stay alone with him. After Paravasu comes back Vishakha explains to him: "Something died inside your father the day the king chose you to be the chief priest. He has been drying up like a dead tree since then. No sap runs in him" (32). On the other hand, lust consumes Raibhya. Commenting on his behaviour after Paravasu's departure for the *Yajna*, he expresses himself thus, "the swarm of dogs sniffing around by daughter-in-law's bottom keeps me in good shape" (29). These words speak volumes about his feelings for his son and his wife. Moreover, it is only with his permission that Paravasu wants to see his own wife Vishakha. On seeing him back with his wife, Raibhya seems to burn with sexual jealousy, "You disgust me, you and the bitch of yours. I am going out." On the other hand, he goes to the extent of killing Yavakri simply because he seduced his daughter-in-law. But Paravasu takes it otherwise: he says his father has killed him only to disturb the Yajna which is at the last stage, "He killed Yavakri. . . . Not to punish Yavakri, but to be even with me." Then he kills his father and admits that he had to attend to him "before he went any farther" (33).

Existentialism

Among the European playwrights Sartre and Camus have influenced Girish Karnad the most; the existential element is a natural feature of Karnad's mode of thinking. Existentialism, which is not a philosophy in the real sense of the word but a mode of thinking, or an attitude, manifested itself after the World War I. It is actually a revival of the thought of Soren Kierkegaard, the Danish writer, who made it current when he realized 'that the individual must be saved as an individual.' He felt that man's existence is in danger from the orthodox religious system and from the industrial and technological age, and, also from the forces of nature that treat him as an object of scientific investigation. The views of the existentialists may vary from each other but an individual and his freedom remain their common interest:

> The common interest which unites existentialist philosophers is the interest in human freedom. They are all of them interested in the world considered as the environment of man, who is treated as a unique object of attention, because of his power to choose his own course of action. What his problem of choice amounts to and how it is to be described. . . . So existentialism is essentially a protest against those forces that tend to reduce human beings and the inner realities of the mind to insignificant proportions.[7]

Due to the influence of Camus and Sartre on Karnad, his characters seem to live in an 'empty' and 'meaningless universe.' They suffer from despair and feeling of nothingness. The more they act to assert themselves the more alienated they get.

In *Yayati* almost all the major characters from the beginning to the end of play suffer from existentialist feeling. Devyani despite her best efforts fails to free herself from it. As Sharmishtha, her childhood friend, tells Yayati that Devyani was broken after Kutch, the man she intensely loved, deserted her. After being deserted by him she "dried up into a thorn" (26) and for many days she could not come out of her house. After being denied love by Kutch, she indulges in abnormal behaviour. She hates everything she comes across. One day Sharmishtha accompanies her for swimming in the river and a lotus flower touches her face. Feeling furious, she crushes it to pieces with one hand. Her inner fury comes out and she lashes out at the lotus flower. The lotus-wine which her hair had entangled with is uprooted in fraction of a second. Devyani, "who would pull an ant biting at her foot softly" (29), can uproot a lotus and destroy it. When she learns that she no more belongs to Kutch, the violence in her overpowers her.

Devyani's second effort to get rid of her alienation comes in the form of her friendship with Sharmishtha, "the friendship between us had deepened." (29) They start staying together. But one day their friendship comes to an end when it occurs to Devyani that Sharmishtha has forgotten her low social status compared to her. This incident snaps their mutual relationship. Perhaps she fails to find the desired satisfaction and joy even in Sharmishtha's company and her low caste becomes a pretext. Then she creates the illusion that Yayati, the king, loves her for her beauty. In Yayati she finds new hope when he pulls her out from a well and makes her his queen. But when she discovers that he has shared bed with Sharmishtha, she again loses control over herself. She leaves Yayati forever though she knows, "To forget is not so easy. . . . Who will roll from door to door as a prostitute? I am yet to see it." Now, she has the full realization that she will have to live alone and isolated in her life to come as she has desperately failed in her effort to create an illusion of her own identity.

The next existentialist character in the play is the king himself. Yayati, like Devyani, is deserted by his own wife who fascinated him much. She cannot give him the joy he expects from her. He says that he married her but she could not give him even a little peace. She was only her son's mother. She deceived Yayati and his son by leaving them alone. The relationship between Yayati and Devyani is the result of Yayati's disappointment with his own life. But she too cannot provide him the desired peace. Then the seduction of Sharmishtha is one more attempt on his part to get rid of his inner isolation. But it further alienates him as he, cursed by Devyani's father for deceiving his daughter, loses his youth and turns old. When he finds that his subjects have flatly refused to accept his old age, he literally cries and begs his son for help. Yayati's cries and his falling over the feet of his son remind us of Muhammad who too cries like a child after feeling alienated from all sides. None of his subjects is ready to take the curse on his head. Finally, Puru comes forward to own his father's old age. But amongst his wife, Devyani, Sharmishtha or his son none can help him.

As regards the other characters, none seems free of existential alienation. Puru is restless since his childhood. He is always feeling desperate to assert his existence somehow. Exchanging his youth with his father's old age can be viewed as an attempt in that direction. But this sacrifice also fails to bring any solution to his problem. Like him, his newly wedded wife is not free from the feeling of alienation even after marriage. When she is looking sad, her attendant says that sadness shouldn't be in the girl like her at such a young age. The feeling of despair surrounds even the palace she lives in. It looks "forlorn" all around. Scared of the atmosphere of despair she does not like to meet the people who have come to receive her outside. The people standing out have sadness "spread over their faces." In order to escape the feeling of boredom for a while, she asks Swaranlata, her attendant, to narrate some story to fill the 'gap.' But Swaranlata has her own tale of woes. She says that she too was married like her and she led the marital life for ten years but it was always without peace. One morning she was left alone by her husband to lead her life on her own. She is still in search of peace which remains an illusion for her. Her present miserable life is revealed in the opening scene when she is with Devyani. The grief in her spurts out against Sharmishtha. She holds her responsible for making her life miserable, "That whore . . . had you not stopped me I would have pulled her by hair," (10) says she to Devyani. Her life as an attendant in Yayati's palace has made suffering "a habit for her." She rightly says, "Suffering like the love for enjoyment becomes a habit. Once you are one with it, you can't live without it." Moreover, there is always a "storm" blowing "inside her": she laughs and talks only to "to cover up her real self," (11) confesses Swaranlata. Sharmishtha is also fighting against the feeling of nothingness in her life. She is not only living with the cries and curses of Devyani and Swaranlata at present, her past also is not free from grief. She fails to recover herself from the shock of being rejected in love by Devyani. This experience always torments her internally. Nothing can be more tormenting for her than becoming the slave of her old friend. She becomes her slave in the same palace. She can't even go back to her parents as Devyani won't release her from this slavery. As a last resort, she offers herself to Yayati.

Admitting existential alienation in Muhammad Tughlaq, Christine Gomez remarks, "Girish Karnad's play *Tughlaq* works out its protagonist's progressive alienation with existential overtones. Like Camus's *Caligula*, *Tughlaq* may also be seen as a play that deals with an alienated outsider figure, estranged at various levels, from society and the individuals around him, from traditional religion, from existence and human predicament in this world and from himself." Tughlaq's alienation begins to appear from Scene II in the play. He informs Sheikh Imam-ud-din about the "Surrounding Void" which sometimes pushes itself into his souls and starts "pushing out every light burning there" (20). He starts cursing every one around him feeling that he is not being understood. His agony is better explained when he cries out that he couldn't bear the "walls" any more. He felt that he needed an audience to confess his self pity to. He can't sleep, nor can he read and always feels restless. His inner suffering won't let him be at peace. Once he wished and prayed for no sleep but now he longs to have a wink of it: "This change he can't believe now" (195).

His alienation is manifested in two ways: first in his manipulation of the people for his own ends treating them as mere objects; second, in his failure to develop communication even with his close ones. The reason is that he believes in his own strength too much. To him, his own existence is more important and he seems to believe in the notion that 'existence precedes essence.' The existentialist belief that man's knowledge got from existence is superior to any knowledge that is theoretical, guides

Muhammad's way. Sovideva does not look at others for the welfare of his subjects. He believes in his own strength and says, "no one can go far on his knees. I cannot afford to crawl. I have to gallop" (164). He refuses to accept the *Koran* as the only receptacle of truth. But this self-confidence does not help him for long.

From his alienation and anguish stems the cruelty and bloodshed which he adopts as a measure to fill the "void" around him. 'Anguish' in existential philosophy, "is the reaction of a man who has had a vision of the absurd and realizes the nothingness, the void that is at the centre of existence."[8] And cruelty and tyranny help the alienated to overcome his sense of absurdity of human existence. Muhammad, too, starts with killing every one close to him including his stepmother and ends with violence only. When he doubts the intentions of Ain-ul-Malik and Barani proposes to excuse him as he is a man who worships God; Muhammad pays no heed to him and clearly says, "traitor is traitor and he must be crushed?" (159). In fact killing somebody does not mean anything to him; hence he feels no need to confirm his doubts.

When Muhammad makes announcement to shift his capital from Delhi to Daulatabad, he has no regrets of any sort for rendering his own people homeless. He orders that every one must leave Delhi: "Not a light should be seen in the windows of Delhi. Not a wisp of smoke should rise from its chimney. Nothing but empty graveyard of Delhi will satisfy me." His every sentence starts with 'Not' or 'Nothing' hinting at the sense of nothingness prevailing upon him. When Shihabudin plans to kill him in prayer but is caught, the cruelty in Muhammad comes to the fore. He at once turns red with anger. Looking at the furious Muhammad advancing towards him with a dagger in his hand, Shihabudin says, "Go on with your killing. . . . You want to solve all problems with the flash of a dagger" (184). The cruel Muhammad remains unmoved by Shihabudin's words. He says that he could have killed him with a sword, but he liked him "too much." Then he starts stabbing him frenziedly. He kills Shihabudin with such ferocity that even the soldiers holding the body turn their faces away. When Barani tries to cover the dead body with a silken cloth, Muhammad casts the cloth away and shouts, "Don't cover him, Barani. I want my people to see his wounds." Then he orders that everyone involved in the murder-attempt be hanged; and, "stuff their heads with straw and hang them up in the palace yard. Let them hang there for a week." It appears that he wants to quench his thirst for peace with human blood which further leads to his restlessness. He kills the Sheikh by making him his envoy, killing two birds with one stone. When he finds that his own stepmother has poisoned his associate Najib, the tyrant in him dries up all the son-like emotions and he orders her to be stoned to death. He creates the atmosphere of terror in his kingdom. Out of fear, as he is informed, four Amirs leave his kingdom and the fifth commits suicide. But the king won't let them escape and he orders that if the Amirs don't come back, 'I shall be sorry for their families." His mother questions his pursuit for endless killings and reminds him how his kingdom has become a "kitchen of deaths." Muhammad defends his spree of cruelty saying these are not "futile deaths." They "give him what he wanted, i.e., "power, strength to shape my thought, strength to act, strength to recognize myself." (204). Muhammad knows fully well that under his command, his soldiers have "butchered everyone in sight." Even his friend Barani's mother has fallen victim to this violence. He accepts that he is "responsible for that massacre" (203). Thus search for identity through cruelty and bloodshed makes him a typical existentialist character. The despair and 'nothingness,' which he has been undergoing throughout his life, overpower him at the end. His anxiety-ridden-self compels him to make a frank confession, "my skin drips with blood and I don't know how much of it is mine and how much of others" (205). Now he feels like "wandering naked" in a desert. He started with prayer that was a must for every Muslim, but now he feels himself as a "pig rolling in the gory mud." During the days of shifting the capital to Daulatabad there is an atmosphere of screaming, burning of houses and killing of people. Aazam informs Aziz of the scene outside where the streets are "full of dead bodies, corpses and flies" (211). Thus, death and destruction coupled with starvation and cruelty mark the scene everywhere.

The element of cruelty and bloodshed is also the characteristic feature of *Tale-Danda*. The Sharanas, who do not believe in the caste-system and stand for equality in all human beings, become an eyesore for the king Bijjala who sees threat to his throne in their slogan of equality. He tolerates them when they are limited to preaching only. As he learns about the inter-caste marriage arranged by the Sharanas, it outrages him. Gundanna informs how the king had adopted oppressive measures to finish the Sharanas' movement. He says that the king's soldiers have arrested Haralayya and have taken him to the city square for punishment. Then the city people watched that the Sharanas' eyes were being plucked and they were being dragged through the streets tied to elephants' legs: "torn limbs along the lanes, torn-entrails—they died screaming." Terrified by oppression in the kingdom, Kalavati, the mother of the newly wedded girl, runs away with her daughter and son-in-law. Her husband is killed and she "ran down the street screaming and no one knows where she is, perhaps in a lake or in a well" (82).

Sovideva, the king's son, who is also against the Sharanas, orders his men to "bury them alive" and "hack them to pieces" (90). After his father's death, he gives a free hand to violence against the Sharanas despite his mother's warning against their power. At the end he sees people rushing through the streets "howling" and "screaming" and there is nobody to look after them. The messenger, too, informs Sovideva that the royal guards have gone on a rampage and have started looting the city, "temples are being sacked," "trading houses torched" and the whole city "reels under gruesome tales of rape, murder and rioting." (89) Calling the Sharanas the tribe of snakes, he orders his men to annihilate them and "cause their progeny." They are ordered to pursue the Sharanas and not to let them escape: "Men, women and children cut them down." He directs them to set the hounds after them, "Burn their houses, their books" and "their voices should be stilled for ever" (90). Thus, there is violence all around which is further added to by Jagadeva's killing Bijjala and gagging his bodyguard.

Nagamandala is another powerful portrayal of agony and anguish. It also presents a tale of woe and despair manifested through the character of Rani. Rani, the protagonist, suffers from the feeling of loneliness and agony even after marriage. Appanna, her husband, visits her only for his meals, otherwise she is always confined within the four walls of her house. She is not allowed to look outside. When Appanna is away from his home, Kurudavva, the old friend of Appanna's mother, visits his house and finds Rani locked in a room. Appanna learns about this visit and does not like it. He brings a watch-dog to guard Rani against any outsider who comes to see her. Thus, she is tortured in every way and her problem gets complicated when she fails to distinguish between the two selves of Appanna: one who visits her bedroom at night and the other who is cruel and inhuman during the day. When she tells him that she feels "frightened" alone at night, she is only snubbed: "just keep to yourself and no one will bother you" (28). She is ordered to bring rice and there ends her meeting with her husband. She feels lonely and miserable and craves for parental affection like a child. She moans "Oh mother, father!" in her sleep. During day time she remembers her favourite nursery tale and daydreams an eagle taking her to her parents who cares for her affectionately. But coming back to the real world, she becomes sad again. She is found sobbing endlessly as she unfolds her tale of suffering to Kurudavva. She says that she is "bored to death" as there is "no one to talk to." She feels frightened and cannot have "a wink at night." Feeling tired of her suffering; she is ready even to jump into a well. One day when Appanna is at home and Rani is away just for a second to pour out the mixture prepared from the root, it offends him: "He slaps her hard. Rani collapses to the floor. He does not look at her again. He just pulls the door shut, locks it from outside and goes away." Thus, he has nothing for his wife but "just cold contempt." She is treated only as a lifeless creature.

After the watch-dog is killed, a mongoose is brought to guard Rani against any outsider. The romantic moments with her husband during day time was already a dream for Rani. Now she also "loses her nights with Naga. He also stops visiting her after his encounter with mongoose. Now she experiences total alienation and anxiety:

> But my real anxiety began as the evening approached. I would merely lie here, my eyes shut tight. What is there to see after all? The same walls. The same roof. As the afternoon passed my whole being got focused in my ears . . . now he will come. Suppose he doesn't tonight? Suppose it is all dream? Every night the same anxiety. The same cold feeling, a deep anxiety (50).

When she is made pregnant by Naga but is ordered not to disclose it to anybody, it pains her much. She curses Naga and calls him "cold-blooded" and says, "You can't be a human." Finding him unhappy with her pregnancy she cries and threatens him of abortion: "I may find a sharp instrument in the kitchen—a blade, a knife." Thus, even her pregnancy fails to bring any change. She doesn't know what to do, "Laugh? Cry? Bang my head against the wall?" When her husband learns about her conception he also calls her a "harlot" and asks: "Who did she go with her sari off?" (52). Now day or night makes no difference to her. Her pregnancy takes away the only charm she had for nights. Along with the displeasure of his lover, she earns the ire of her husband. If Naga asks her to keep her pregnancy a secret, Appanna threatens her in the name of the Village-Elders. He is sure that they will throw the child she is carrying into "boiling oil" along with her as she has turned promiscuous. Rani's words tell a lot about her agony: "Why are you humiliating me like this? Why are you stripping me naked in front of the whole village? Why don't you kill me instead? I would have killed myself. But there is not even a rope in the house for me to use." (53). She is ready to take poison and meet her end like the dog and the mongoose at her door to avoid the public humiliation. But none listens to her.

In *Hayavadana* too, almost all the characters are victims of alienation and agony but Devadatta is the worst sufferer. Kapila and Devadatta are alienated due to their incomplete personalities. If Kapila is only 'the body' Devadatta is only 'the mind' and thus they need each other for their completion. As M. Sarat Babu says, "Actually their friendship is based on the fact that they depend on each other for what each lacks and both suffer from self-alienation." Unlike Devadatta, Kapila has never looked at any girl nor proposed to anyone as he lacks the emotional self. He has the physical courage needed to propose to Padmini and he shows it on Devadatta's behalf. Devadatta, on the other hand, has fallen in love fifteen times in a period of two years and Padmini is his sixteenth love. If Kapila is the physical self, Devadatta is the emotional self.

From the very beginning Devadatta and Kapila live together and love each other: "Two friends they were one mind one heart" (82). But when Devadatta sees Padmini he falls for her. His attraction towards Padmini reveals that Kapila's love has not given him the feeling of completeness. That is why he is ready to sacrifice his arms and head to gods if he succeeds in marrying her. In his attraction for her he simply says that he is helpless. As they start living together after marriage, Kapila becomes an eye-sore for him. The same old friend appears to be the spoiler of his marital joys and becomes the source of despair for Devadatta. Whenever his wife questions his intentions about Kapila, it "burns his insides" (92). When Kapila poetically describes the Fortunate

Lady flower brought by him on their way to Ujjain, Devadatta shows no interest at all. He has seen with his own eyes how Padmini was lost in staring at Kapila when he goes to fetch the flower for her. In an 'Aside' he says "Look! Let your guts burn out. . . . Let your lungs turn to ash but don't turn away. Look—and don't scream. Strangle your agony. But look deep into these eyes—Look until those peacock flames burn out the blindness in you. Don't be a coward now" (96). As Padmini asks him to put Kapila's imagination in his poetry, he says: "Shall we go? It is quite late" It is evident that he is aware of his being 'late' now. When they leave for the temple of Rudra, he bids them goodbye. He blesses them both, "good-bye, Kapila. Good-bye, Padmini. May Lord Rudra bless you? You are two pieces of my heart—live happily together. I shall find my happiness in that (agonized)." It shows that he is torn between the outer and the inner pulls. He pretends to be happy to see them together but internally he is unable to bear the pain of being isolated from his dear ones. His suicide in the temple of Kali is an attempt to escape the agony. But after he resumes his life with the body of Kapila, Padmini again leaves him and reaches the forest where Kapila is living. Failing to face his alienation for the second time, he suggests to Kapila that they should kill each other. Even Padmini's child is not free from this feeling of alienation. No human being interests him, his only interest is in the lifeless dolls. He refuses to communicate with anyone around him and doesn't let anybody touch his dolls. This suggests his absorption in a world of make-believe from which he has no desire to emerge. The sight of the laughing horse, however, suddenly breaks the barriers, as his innate child-like sense of wonder and delight in the strange is roused in a flash, and it is this laughter that restores him to normalcy, after which he drops the dolls. *Hayavadana* thus presents a typical existentialist anguish but does not stop an existentialist despair, the play suggests a strategy for the achievement of integrity in a world inevitably cursed with absurdity and irrationality.

The Fire and the Rain puts forth Yavakri who is a victim of jealousy, anxiety and the same feeling of alienation. He burns with jealousy when he learns that his father is deprived of the honour which has been bestowed upon Raibhya, his uncle. He vows to acquire the knowledge of Vedas direct from the gods, only to use it to give vent to his feeling of revenge against Raibhya. After spending ten years in a forest for gaining knowledge he, as if restless to take revenge upon Raibhya, comes directly to Vishakha, Raibhya's daughter-in-law. Burning with the fire of revenge, he plans the occasion to seduce her and bring disgrace to Raibhya. When she is not willing to talk to a stranger and suggests to him to see her father-in-law if necessary, he says "It's not the need to speak to him that brings me here."[9] He indirectly hints that his meeting has an evil design. But she fails to see through it and falls in his trap. The devil in Yavakri makes him exploit his old beloved emotionally:

> You want to hit me? Go ahead. . . . You and Indra. That's right. The presiding deities of my life. It is because of you two that I have avoided women altogether until now. Conserved my seed like you conserve your water. Now as I sit in front of you. I want to betray Indra—he left me ignorant. (15)

Then jealousy turned into treachery provokes him to seduce her. Even the metaphysical knowledge and meetings with gods fail to make him forget his bitter past. The feeling of jealousy always haunts him and his desire for revenge never dies. Vishakha rightly says that the whole world may be singing his praises but he has not "grown up." And rightly so, he is pre-determined to catch Raibhya "by his scrotum and squeeze it so hard that he couldn't even squirm." Even Vishakha's total yielding to him in love fails to move him. Rather, he says that if she had not willingly yielded to him, he would have used force. For this moment he feels that his "entire life has rushed headlong" (29). He confesses that he loves her and for her sake he has not accepted any other woman in his life. But he cannot forgive her father-in-law for her sake. At last we see him running, gasping and falling down to escape the Brahman-Rakshasa but to no avail. Wanting to torment and kill others, he himself gets killed at the end.

As Yavakri is jealous and revengeful Vishakha is feeling altogether alienated. Like Yavakri she too feels "hungry for words." First she was left alone by Yavakri himself when he left her for penance. Then she married Paravasu who also left her after some time. Now she is to live with his father-in-law who is already burning with the feeling of anger and humiliation. So, she is always in search of someone who can "speak" to her and terminate her alienation. She won't reject Yavakri outrightly as she does not want to miss out more chance for her joy. She confesses that she could not walk on because she knows "that hunger well." She frankly says "You are hungry for words and so am I. So let's talk" (15); she has been living in the hermitage "parched" and "wordless" like a "she-devil." After one year of marriage with Paravasu, the question of her happiness "receded into the background." After Paravasu left for Yajna and was acting as the chief priest of the fire sacrifice, he has not visited her ever since. She also knows that he cannot leave the sacrifice midway though she is waiting for his arrival. Fed up with her loneliness, she says:

> But in all these seven years he hasn't come back. I know he can't. But I look forward to having him home once the seven years are over. Alone, I have become dry like tinder. Ready to burst into flames at a breath. To burn things around me down to the slightest chance. (16)

Even her old lover fails to bring any relief to her. Rather, he adds to her sufferings with his second meeting.

Life without love has led her to a feeling that every man confines himself to woman's body alone but the woman is beyond it. She rightly tells Yavakri, "My husband and you! He left no pore in my body alone. And you . . . you think a woman is only a pair of half-formed breasts" (16). After meeting Yavakri when she moves to her place her clothes are torn and her back is covered with mud, her father-in-law calls her "filthy" and a "buffalo rolling in mud." He grabs her by her hair and starts beating her, kicking her head. Arvasu, failing to witness the scene intervenes but cannot check the violent Raibhya. When she confesses that Yavakri had come to see her alone Raibhya's behaviour reminds us of Rani's husband in *Nagamandala*. Like him Raibhya shouts: "You whore—you roving whore, I could reduce you to ashes—turn you into a fistful of dust—with a simple curse. But let that husband of yours handle you. . . . Let him clean up his own shit!" (20). Vishakha's suffering and anxiety mounts up when she discovers that Yavakri had planned everything to take revenge on her father-in-law. This pains her much and she repents over her yielding to him. She expresses herself thus: "I was so happy this morning. You were so good so warm. I wanted to envelop you in everything I could give. It was more as a mother that I offered my breasts to you. . . . Why is life so contrary Yavakri? One thinks one has stepped onto a bit of solid ground—a little haven—and the earth gives way" (24).

When her husband is back in his hermitage at night he makes her all the more alienated by not responding to her questions. He also wants to be the equal of Indra by shedding all human weaknesses. She begs him to be as he was before Indra got into him. But she receives no answer from her husband except silence with which she is already fed up. She cries at her lot: "I shouldn't ask. I should be silent. And you, in any case, will be silent. My silence again will be followed by yours. Silence endlessly repeated. Perhaps that too will describe a whole universe. But I am sick of silence." (32) When her husband fails to break it, she asks a favour from him, i.e., to kill her: she prefers death to her life without "words." This is how almost every major character in Karnad is the victim of alienation and despair.

Treatment of Religion

Karnad's treatment of religion and religious ideas in his plays further proves him a modern playwright. Religion in Marxian view, according to *Encyclopaedia of Religion* is "the opium that people take to dull their pain and give them dreams." In this regard Leo Chester's remark is noteworthy: "The only true solution is precisely where human judgment sees no solution. Otherwise, what need would we have to God? We turn towards God only to obtain the impossible. As for the possible, men suffice."[10] In Sigmund Freud, too, religion is "universal obsessional neurosis of humanity." Freud holds that God is the "exalted father" and longing for the father is the root of the need for religion: "Religion could be reduced to a humanity neurosis and its great power could be explained in the same way as the neurotic compulsion of some of our patients."[11] About the origin and nature of religion he says, "A large number of human beings undertake in common to create an illusion for happiness and a protection against suffering by means of a chimerical development of reality. Hence, we must define the religions of mankind as such mass chimera." Thus in his attempt to make something which can give him a hope of shelter or protection, man creates the image of God. Freud calls religion a derivation from the Oedipus complex: "Religion is a general compulsion-neurosis like that of a child and derives from the Oedipus complex, the relation to the father." Man feels helpless before the forces of nature, so he moulds them in the image of man but not as men who are his equal but with the features of his father: a superior being. This image of 'a superior being' springs out of man's necessity and helplessness. This is best portrayed in *Tughlaq* and *Hayavadana.*

Muhammad, the main character in *Tughlaq*, in his endeavour to be a successful ruler, becomes helpless and appears neurotic at times. He meets failures at all fronts and the men around seem to turn hostile to him. He looks to God as the last resort for his peace of mind. Muhammad's idea of God appears to arise from the same 'helplessness' and 'neurosis.' He realizes that he has too big a responsibility to perform for his public. But he has not been able to do anything and his life is too small. For that he prays to God to save him from sleep as he does not want to waste away the "one life, one body" (155) he has got. Like a Hindu he cannot believe in the theory of recurring births and he cannot postpone his remaining projects for the next life. In order to materialize his dreams he exhausts each and every source but the result always goes against him. The man he trusts most turns against him in no time. Ain-ul-Mulk whom he made Governor of Avadh for crushing rebels and restoring law begins to assume himself to be a God almost. When the king sends him a letter for being the Governor of the Deccan and to leave immediately, Ain-ul-Mulk takes it as "a knife in his back" and thus turns against Muhammad. Similarly, Sheikh Imam-ud-din publicly calls him a murderer and announces that the king has forfeited the right to rule by murdering his father and brother, that too during prayer time. Thus there is a widespread sense of dissatisfaction among his subjects. Muhammad is aware that he is charged with murder, as he shares it with Barani: "Do you think really that parricide is a little thing! And parricide? And the pollution of prayer? It's not what people say, Barani, it is their crooked minds that horrify me. Look at my own mother . . . she won't talk to me now—she believes I killed them . . . even this stepmother of mine thinks I am a murderer. (157-58)

This constant worry that he is not proving an ideal king and the people do not accept him as a competent ruler, makes Muhammad neurotic. Each of his plans turns overboard. The more he tries to be near his destination, the farther it moves. When he informs Shihabudin and the Amirs about introducing copper currency, it shocks everyone. Shihabudin doubts if a copper coin can have the same value as a silver one. When Amir calls him mad in an 'Aside' but tries to cover it up saying that people won't accept paper currency, Muhammad's neurosis spurts out: "Then why not say it aloud because people are afraid, will you mistrust me too? Laugh at me if you like, criticize me, but please don't distrust me. I can order you to obey me but tell me, how do I gain your full support for that. If you don't understand me, ask me to explain myself and I'll do it. If you don't understand my explanations, bear with me in patience until I can show you the results. But please don't let me down. I beg you. I'll kneel before you if you wish, but please do not let me go off my head. (*Then he kneels before the Amirs who almost recoil at his sudden gesture*)" (182). Shihabudin feels embarrassed at this. He reminds Muhammad that it is not for a king to kneel down as he is only to command. Getting up and picking up the copy of Koran, Muhammad asks Shihabudin and the Amirs to take an oath to support him.

Muhammad turns neurotic in his attempt to please his subjects. Sometimes he roars like a king and sometimes kneels like a beggar. He can kill a man without a tinge of mercy and at the very next moment he cries like a child. First he goes on stabbing Shihabudin, then throws his dagger away and asks Barani, "Why must it happen Barani? Are all those I trust condemned to go down in history as traitors? What is happening? Tell me Barani, will my reign be nothing more than a tortured scream which will stab the night and melt away in the silence" (185). Then he is seen "trembling all over." In the next moment after lamenting over what is happening around him, he orders to behead everybody who is involved in the conspiracy of his murder. He orders to stuff Shihabudin's body with straw and hang it up for the public to see. After the fit is over he is again very rational and advises Najib to make a public announcement that Shihabudin had died while saving the Sultan from the nobles. Thus, the neurotic Muhammad kills Shihabudin and declares him a martyr, orders to vacate Delhi within a fortnight "to see only the graveyard of Delhi," exiles prayer as he finds that the prayers too are ridden with disease but reverses his decision soon making prayer obligatory for every Muslim later.

Even after five years of shifting from Delhi to Daulatabad, Muhammad's neurosis haunts him. It comes to light when he is talking to a young watchman at the fort of Daulatabad. He feels nostalgic about his youth when he was eighteen years old. When the watchman fails to perceive Muhammad's philosophical utterance, he feels upset over his poor understanding: "(incensed) you don't understand! You don't understand! Why do you live? Why do you corrupt the air with your diseased breath? (Suddenly calm) I'm sorry. It's my turn to apologize. It isn't your fault. You are also one of them" (194). Sometimes he is a philosopher, a scholar and sometimes an irrational man cursing and rebuking everyone around him. At the end, he is no more a cruel king but a man of poor conscience, feeling apologetic before his watchman. When he says that he is suffering from insomnia and Barani asks him to see a *hakim*, Muhammad rightly questions, "What can a hakim do?" in his case. He expects some panacea from Barani as he feels that he is entangled in the "honeycomb of diseases." As Barani hints that he belongs to the company of learned men and he should desist from killing others, Mohammad again laughs neurotically. He makes a frank confession of his longing for some supernatural help for peace. He "often thought of myself to give up that futile see-saw struggle and go to Mecca, sit there by the Kaba and search for the peace which Daulatabad has not given me" (196). But that too is not easy for him, he feels completely helpless: "But it is not that easy. It is not as easy as leaving the patient in the wilderness because there is no cure of his diseases. Don't you see—this patient? Rocked by fever and crazed by the fear of enveloping vultures, can't be separated from me?" (196) He knows it well that his subjects call him 'mad Muhammad.' When Barani tells him to stop the bloodshed he has indulged in, he declines. In no way he wants to accept that he has been in the wrong over the years.

Muhammad's neurotic behaviour is noticeable at the discovery of Aziz's disguise as a saint. First he turns red with anger but as Aziz explains that a saint is no match for a washerman when it comes to washing others' filth, Muhammad suddenly bursts into a guffaw. There is a "slight hysterical tinge" in this laughter. First he is found exploding on Aziz ordering him "to hold his tongue" but the next moment he laughs aloud and calls him a genius. To everybody's surprise he sends Aziz on a mission to Khusrou-Malik appointing him as an officer in his army. Of his neurotic and resultant relationship with God, his view is: "Anyway, what do all these subtle distinctions matter in the blinding madness of the day? . . . all I need now is myself and my madness—madness to prance in a field eaten bare by the scarecrow violence. But I am not alone, Barani. Thank Heaven! For once I am not alone I have a companion to share my madness now—the Omnipotent God! (Tired)." (219-20)

It is only in the moment of agony that Muhammad calls on God. His idea of God emerges from some desperate situations when he has exhausted all his abilities as an individual. Viewed from this angle, the scene where he sentences his mother to death is noteworthy. We see him ordering his stepmother to be stoned to death publicly despite her requests and cries. But he is bent upon giving her the death of a traitor. When his mother is dragged away by his soldiers as ordered by him, Muhammad falls on his knees and clutches his hands to his chest and cries: "God, God, in Heaven, please help me. . . . I started in your path. . . . I started in search of you. . . . Raise me. Clean me. Cover me with your Infinite Mercy. I can only clutch at the hem of your cloak with my bloody fingers and plead. I can only beg—have pity only. I have no one but you now. Only you . . . you . . . you . . . you." (205-6).

Neurotically, he himself is praying when the prayer is banned in his kingdom. He looks to God for help as his own legs don't bear his burden anymore, "But what else could I do Barani? My legs couldn't hold me up any longer." When Barani thinks he can please him with the news of Ghiyas-ud-Din's visit to their kingdom, Muhammad finds no joy in it. He feels his visit can bring him no peace as he is "teetering on the brink of madness" (206) He is trying to pray but he can't as God too seems to evade him. Then he shouts that he actually doesn't deserve the 'madness of God' because of the sins he has been committing on his subjects. Feeling dumb before Barani's arguments proving him responsible for the chaos around him, Muhammad warns him that he is not alone as the "omnipotent God" is with him. Here Barani wishes to leave him as he smells further chaos in his kingdom. Muhammad, feeling sleepy, permits him to go but requests him to "pray" for him before he leaves.

Search for some God-like figure in the moments of helplessness is also a typical feature of *Hayavadana*. Devadatta, despite his intellectual qualities and rich ancestral background does not deem himself fit to be Padmini's husband. He invokes Kali and Lord Rudra to help him. He swears, "If I ever get her as my wife, I will sacrifice my two arms to the Goddess Kali, I shall sacrifice my head to Lord Rudra" (85). At this Kapila starts feeling that he must be in a serious situation otherwise he is not the type to talk with such violence. After he succeeds in marrying Padmini, the most desperate moment for him arrives when Padmini and Kapila go out to the temple of Rudra leaving him alone. When they are late in coming back, again he thinks of Lord Rudra. He starts begging for "strength from him" (Lord Rudra). He looks to the god for some supernatural help like Muhammad Tughlaq. He prays: "(agonized) Give me strength, Lord Rudra. My father gives me courage. I am already trembling. I'd never thought I would be so afraid. Give me courage, father, strengthen me" (98). Then he walks to the temple of Kali. Now when he has no hope of any human help from anybody: both human sources of help have ditched him, he expects help from some metaphysical power. More interesting is the fact that in his happy moments he forgets everything about his promises made to the deities. Only now he remembers, "Bhavani, Bhairavi, Kali, Durga, Mahamaya, Mother of all Nature. I had forgotten my promise to you. Forgive me, Mother. You fulfilled the deepest cravings of my life. You gave me Padmini and I forgot my word. Forgive me." (88-99) As a last resort he looks for help to the temple again after he is deserted by his dear ones. Before he cuts off his head in the temple of Kali, his state of mind is conveyed by Kapila thus: "You've cut off your head! . . . Were you so angry with me? Did you feel such contempt for me—such abhorrence? And in your anger you forgot. Did you despise me so much. You spurned me in this world. Accept me as your brother at least in the next." (100)

It is evident that Devadatta is full of 'anger' and contempt at the time of his death. Feeling too weak to face the situation, he kills himself. Padmini also feels that he is "too weak to have gone far." Obviously, it is due to the lack of some inner strength that Devadatta looks to some supernatural help as does Muhammad in *Tughlaq*. In this way the idea of religion and God in Girish Karnad is compatible with the ideology of modern thinkers like Freud and Marx.

Thus Girish Karnad delves deep into the ancient myths and legends in an attempt to spell out modern man's dilemma. Upon the mythological canvas he draws the contours of contemporary reality: "Man has been his chief interest, with his glories, defeats, dreams, aspirations and frustrations. It is this angle of human interest that gives it an element of contemporaneity, despite the mythological canvas, Girish Karnad's interest in man is well-defined."

Unity of tradition and modernity becomes the hallmark of his plays. The present for him grows out of the past and hence it cannot be dealt with in isolation and viewed as a separate entity. The past, to Girish Karnad, never dies but lives through the legends and folk tales. Since these mythical tales are the stories of elemental human passions, in every narration they get new meaning. As regards the historically true incidents, Karnad again seems to believe in the notion that history repeats itself. The historical incidents are also eternal in character as they occur and recur with agents different in name only. The historical events in Karnad mirror the current political, religious and social happenings. Every play is the story of a new problem of the modern man. Yayati and Puru in Yayati picturize the relationship between every father and son where the father expects his son to make sacrifice for him and the younger generation suffers because of the fixations of the old one. Rani of *Nagamandala* and Padmini of *Hayavadana* are there in our present society. They suffer because of the male-chauvinistic attitude and the hard and unbreakable social institutions as of marriage. These modern Indian women become permanent victims of sufferings because of their failure to break the social laws. Both ways they are the sufferers: whether they abide by these social dictates or violate them. Muhammad Tughlaq and the king Bijjala hint at the present Indian rulers who use the religious biases for their political gains. Otherwise, they don't believe in any religion and their only religion is 'Power.' They are always wearing a mask which changes as the situation demands. This socio-political concern takes the form of socio-religious one in *The Fire and the Rain*. The hypocrisy in politics changes into that of religious practices. In his interview with S. Gulvadi, Karnad defends his inclination towards the past to understand his present:

> Well, if it's only a play about the past, then it is not worth it. The point is: the story may be from the past. But the play must be about the present. Plays must be contemporary. No, I don't deliberately try to make it contemporary subject. If I have contemporary consciousness, it will become modern because I am a modern writer writing about it. If I have no modern consciousness, even if I take a contemporary topic, that will look like a Puranic play. It is not the subject matter that makes it Puranic. It takes the sensibility of the writer. If that sensibility is really modern, if it is contemporary, if it is sensitive to present-day issues, well, you can write *Tale-Danda*. So, the sensibility is never there in the subject. It is there in the

writer. And if I have it, it will be contemporary. If I don't have it, it will not be contemporary.

Truly so, the current theories regarding human behaviour propounded by Sigmund Freud, Karl Marx and the Existentialist thinkers like Jean-Paul Sartre and Albert Camus find expression in oral and folk tales. The plots which have gods and goddesses as characters ridicule the idea of religion and morality in the traditional sense of the word. Karnad's protagonists, despite being traditional, assert their modernity by raising a banner against anything human or superhuman that restricts their freedom. This seems to advocate the modern ideas such as religion as the 'universal-neurosis' or the 'Opium of the masses' and 'existence-precedes-essence' etc.

NOTES

1. Girish Karnad, *Yayati*, trans. B.R. Narayana (New Delhi: Saraswati Printing Press, 1979), p.8. All the quotations have been translated from Hindi to English by the writer.
2. Girish Karnad, *The Fire and the Rain* (New Delhi: Oxford University Press, 1998), p. ix.
3. Girish Karnad, *Tale-Danda* (New Delhi: Paul Press, 1993).
4. Girish Karnad, *Three Plays: Nagamandala, Hayavadana, Tughlaq* (New Delhi: Oxford University Press, 1993).
5. Calvin, S. Hall, *A Primer of Freudian Psychology* (New York: The New American Press, 1957), p. 110.
6. R.S. Woodworth, "Psychoanalysis and Relative Theories," *Contemporary Schools of Psychology* (New York: Bantam, 1970), pp. 70-71.
7. Mary Warnock, *Existentialism* (Great Britain: Oxford University Press, 1977), p. 23.
8. F.N. Maurice Cranston, *Sartre* (Edinburgh & London: Oliver and Boyd, 1962), p. 49.
9. Qtd. Albert Camus, "An Absurd Reasoning," *The Myth of Sisyphus*, trans. Justin O'Brien (Great Britain: Penguin, 1975), p. 37.

10. Sigmund Freud, *The Future of an Illusion*, trans. W.D. Rodson-Scott (London: Hogarth Press, 1928), p. 76.
11. Emil Ludwig, *Dr. Freud: An Analysis and a Warning* (New York: Hellman William, 1947), p.259.

Themes

The time we are living in is a "time of doubt and questioning, of self-search and crisis, of a desperate quest for identity and self-hood.[1] Girish Karnad's plays too are concerned with this 'crisis' and 'quest for identity.' He is always in search for some order or a specific system; this search is perpetual in nature appearing in different forms in his different plays. Karnad's protagonists always aspire for something uncommon in which they hardly succeed. From this eternal struggle branch out some other issues which are decisively modern. The milieu of his plays remains Indian with all its social, religious and political features. The modern man with his psychological problems arising from his complex relationships with others remains the essential concern for Girish Karnad as a playwright. Being Indian he cannot view modern man in complete isolation from the religious and spiritual concerns. In this light, his mythical and historical plots can be examined.

Complexity in human relationships is the theme of Karnad's first play *Yayati*. He establishes that man's caste and his social status colour his behaviour. It is difficult to be judgmental about a man in relation to others as his social priorities keep on influencing his behaviour. This is proved by Devyani and Sharmishtha who love each other so much. Sharmishtha is an 'Asur Kanya' (a girl of low birth) but Devyani despite being from a higher caste (Arya) never ridiculed her and had "immense love" for her, feels Sharmishtha. After being loved by a high caste girl, Sharmishtha begins to feel elevated and starts finding new meaning in her existence. From Devyani she gets whatever she wants. Once she asked for a 'Shankh' (a sea shell) which is made after the liking of Devyani's grandfather, she gives it to her and that too without the knowledge of her father. Even she cannot tolerate Devyani's sharing love with somebody else. She wants to be the sole possessor of her love. One day when they are having a bath together in the same river, Sharmishtha feels that her soul has "grown up." She feels ecstatic about their joyous moments together. But this old friendship comes to an abrupt end when their 'kanchakis' (head cloths) are interchanged, and Devyani's Aryan origin comes to her mind. Suddenly she bursts out: "Only by wearing an Arya girl's 'kanchaki' you are dreaming to be an Arya? As a hungry dog takes the moon for his bread" (23). Feeling angry over Devyani's derogatory remarks, Sharmishtha pushes Devyani, whom she loved "more than life," into a well. Devyani who had forgotten her caste for so long could not see her 'kanchaki' being worn by a low caste girl. Their love turns into hatred and Devyani begins to take sadistic pleasure in torturing Sharmishtha.

What happens to Sharmishtha also happens to Devyani in her relationship with Yayati as his wife. She always felt that he had been fascinated by her beauty only. That's why he married her and made her a queen at first sight. Sharmishtha, however, reiterates that there was a selfish motive behind this marriage. But Devyani would never accept it. It is only when she finds that Yayati has developed physical relationship with Sharmishtha and calls her 'queen' in her presence that she discovers the foul intention of the king. Aggrieved at the treachery of the king, she makes a last-ditch effort to convince him for leaving Sharmishtha forever by sending her to her father. But the king would not give in. At this, Devyani goes back to her father. Similarly, the relationship between Yayati and his son Puru, between Puru and his wife Chitralekha and between Chitralekha and Yayati is much more complex to define. If Yayati wants to be an ideal king he also wants to be an ideal father at the same time, that's why he rejects Chitralekha proposal to accept her as his queen; if Puru wants to be an individual he does not run away from his duty as a son. Similarly, Chitralekha, no doubt, wants a courageous husband but this courage should not be at the cost of her youth.

From the complexity of human relationships in general, Karnad shifts his focus to that of a person in particular in his play *Tughlaq*. Muhammad is such a complex character whom it is difficult to define. He starts as a realist but gradually proves to be a bundle of contradictions. One thing that dominates his character is that he is more concerned with his appearances than what he actually is. So he emerges as a great hypocrite: this trait of his travels from the beginning to the end of the play. In the first scene of the play, we find Aziz winning the suit against him as a Brahmin and being given compensation for his loss by the king's court. We soon learn that it is only a 'show' to project the king as a secular ruler. But at the same time, we cannot deny him being imaginative and very intelligent as he proves himself in some of his deft moves as a king. Even in chess he can easily solve the problem which cannot be solved by the experts like Al-Adli and As-Sarakhi. Above all, he is a learned man "known the world over for knowledge of philosophy and poetry" (55).

According to M.K. Naik, "Karnad projects the curious contradictions in the complex personality of the Sultan who is at once a dreamer and man of action, benevolent and cruel, devout and good."[2] Indeed, his complexity cannot be viewed in isolation from the murder of his own father and brother and that too at the prayer time. When Nazim informs that the Sheikh is in Delhi and he has become the backbone of rebels, very cunningly he says, "Aha, then we should take his blessings before he leaves" (157). When he comes to know that Sheikh calls him a "disgrace to Islam" the king does not display his cards to anybody and very indifferently comments, "Let him babble. He is a saint and it is his privilege" (158). Finally, he does what he himself thinks suitable for the occasion: he very cleverly arranges a meeting between the Sheikh and his public. When none turns up to listen to him, very shrewdly he comments, "Do you think I would have gone to the trouble of arranging this meeting if I didn't want my people to hear you? I don't want my people to be dumb cattle Sheikh Sahib, and I don't claim to be omniscient myself. I am quite willing to learn from you—even eager" (163). Moreover, the whole of Delhi has heard of his "courage and integrity" and so he has invited him, says Muhammad. On the other hand, his soldiers reach each and every door and shut the people inside their houses. Trapping the Sheikh thus, the king makes him feel that the people take him as a king's man: a traitor for them. Now his image as a saint is spoiled for ever. If he wants to save his reputation as a saint and if he actually has some concern for the Muslims he should act as an envoy to the neighbouring king who is planning to attack their kingdom and kill the Muslims. Caught in a critical situation the Sheikh gives in and finally gets killed by the king's own soldiers. When Muhammad's mother moans the death of the Sheikh, he also poses to be highly affected by his death. He cries out, "When men like him die, it is a sin to be alive" (171). Sultan's complexity of character touches new heights when the Sheikh is projected as a martyr and his funeral is arranged as a "great affair" where Sheikh's father is to be treated as the father of a loyal nobleman.

Muhammad's complexity does not end here. We witness his complexity further when an attempt is made by Shihabudin and his men to murder him. Muhammad knows beforehand that Shihabudin has hatched a plan to kill him. But he keeps it a secret till the last moment. He goes on praying unperturbed without bringing any sign of confusion on his face. After the prayer is over, he takes out his sword and pounces upon Shihabudin and kills him. Then he announces to the public that Shihabudin is killed while protecting the king from the rebels in the court. He too is announced a martyr by the king and his father is honoured for his son's bravery. About his dubious character, Ratan Singh's statement is highly appropriate: "I have never seen an honest scoundrel like your Sultan. He murders a man calmly and then actually enjoys the feeling of guilt." (171-72).

The same happens to Aziz when he appears in the guise of Ghiyas-ud-din after killing the latter. The king learns about Ghiyas-ud-din's death but he shows no surprise on seeing someone standing before him as Ghiyas-ud-din. He addresses Aziz as "Your Highness" and does not let him doubt his intention. After his identity is disclosed and he admits that he is actually a 'dhobi' from Shiknar, he very shrewdly orders him to go on acting as Ghiyas-ud-din. He never lets his people know about the fate of the real Ghiyas-ud-din. Instead of punishing Aziz, he recommends his name for appointment as an officer. He says, "Remember, you are still 'his holiness' Ghiyas-ud-din Abbasi and you have to be there to lead the prayer. Be off now" (218). All this proves Muhammad a very complex man. He is a poet, a visionary, a learned man, but above all a cruel king. His hobby is rose-gardening, reading books and playing chess. He is constantly talking about tomorrow, "a new future." His visions are like the visions 'which led Zarathustra or the Buddha'; that's why the view that Tughlaq is basically a visionary, a poet but not a ruler. Actually, he plays different roles on different occasions as a perfect actor. About his character a critic aptly remarks:

> The most striking aspect of Tughlaq's character is the complexity that arises from the dualism of the man and hero. He is at once an idealist, and crafty politician, a humanist and a tyrant, a man who has murdered sleep and is haunted by supernatural solicitations.

Complexity in human relationships is again the major issue in *Hayavadana*. All the characters in this play appear as 'incomplete halves' looking for their completion. Devadatta and Kapila, who are "Rama and Krishna, Krishna and Balrama" (74) for the people, love each other and live together like Devyani and Sharmishtha in *Yayati* as if their existence is interlocked. It is for Devadatta's love that Kapila approaches Padmini. He proposes to her for marriage on Devadatta's behalf and succeeds in it. Now they are like "Rama-Sita-Lakshman" (90). But soon a feeling of dislike takes birth in the mind of Devadatta for his friend Kapila. Devadatta smells the attraction between Kapila and his wife Padmini and starts viewing him as an intruder in his personal life. His hatred for Kapila remains no more a secret and he starts comparing his fast friend Kapila with a dog: "He only has to see her and he begins to wag his tail. Sits up on the hind legs as though he were afraid to let her words fall on the ground: And that pleading in his eyes" (91). Devadatta is angry with his wife also who does not look behind Kapila's love-gestures and enjoys his company, "cannot she really see that?," grudges Devadatta. He feels deceived by both: his friend and his wife. For him, Kapila who was like Lakshman to him is not morally supposed to look at his wife, and Padmini, being a Sita to him, is not expected to develop any liking for his friend. Now Devadatta won't like Kapila to accompany them in their trip to the temple of Ujjain as Kapila's presence pleases him no more. But Padmini won't leave Kapila behind even at the cost of her husband's displeasure. On the pretext of her pregnancy, Devadatta intends to postpone the planned trip but Padmini refuses saying that she has a "steel womb," and he should not worry about her. Here the situation is very interesting i.e. none of the three wants to annoy anyone with a clear yes or no. This ambiguity of behaviour brings complexity in their characters.

Devadatta is never straightforward enough to tell Kapila that he should stop visiting his house and leave the couple alone, nor does he clearly check his own wife. See how he covers up his real feelings towards Kapila, "I'm not upset, Padmini. Kapila isn't merely a friend—he is like my brother. One has to collect merit in seven lives to get a friend like him" (91). Same is in the case of Kapila. He too does not want to make his liking public and annoy his old friend. He tries to maintain both the relationships: as a friend of Devadatta and as a lover of Padmini.

The third character in this triangle is Padmini She, too, is very secretive initially about her liking for Kapila. She does not reject Devadatta outright and proposes direct to Kapila. When Devadatta objects to her attraction for Kapila she says, "Look now. You got annoyed about Kapila. But why? You are my saffron, my marriage thread, my deity. Why should you feel upset" (92). Kapila, too, when he and Padmini are back from the temple of Rudra and find Devadatta missing, shows himself to be more concerned for Devadatta's joy. He repeatedly asserts his sincerity towards him and is almost sure that Devadatta did not like his association with them. He laments having not left them alone if his presence somehow troubled him. But the goddess Kali significantly points out that Kapila is selfish even in his sacrifice as he has sacrificed his head not for her but because of the fear of public humiliation he had to face after his friend's death.

The ambiguity of human relationships is rather aggravated when, with the help of the goddess Kali, Padmini joins the head of Devadatta on Kapila's body and vice-versa. This combination, which is best in its type—the intelligent head of Devadatta and the muscular body of Kapila—should satisfy Padmini in every way. But this never happens. Her liking for Kapila never dies. As Devadatta's body begins to lose the earlier muscular shape and changes according to the transposed head, Padmini begins to miss him. She tells Devadatta, "Your body had that male smell before—I liked it—when we came back from the temple of Kali—you used to smell so manly" (113). Sometimes to console herself and Devadatta, she says that she does not want to have him back. It does not matter, she says, if Devadatta is losing his muscles, "What does it matter that you are losing again, that you are losing your muscles? . . . Kapila is gone out of my life forever, I won't let him come back again" (118-19). But it does not turn out to be true. His past haunts her for ever. She begins to recite a lullaby to her son about a soldier and she dreams of a man who is not her husband. She wants to resist the memories of Kapila and pledges: "I won't let him come back again." But later, she herself goes to him in the forest. She can't forget Kapila; she feels sad when she learns from her maid that her mother has died. With the passage of time she becomes rather restless to know: "What could he be doing now? Where could he be? Could his body be fair still and his face dark?" (119).

In pursuit of her desire to see once again the 'changed' Kapila, she succeeds in finding him in a forest. She learns that even Kapila is not satisfied with his new self. He too has "no peace," "no salvation," but he fears going back again. On seeing Padmini he says, "I thought I had won this long and weary battle? Why did you have to pursue me. . . . What do you want now? Another head, another suicide?" (125). Finally, he begs her to do him a favour, i.e., "Go back, back to Devadatta—He is your husband. . . . I beg of you" (125). At the end, Padmini has a feeling that Kapila and Devadatta both are the winners and she is a loser. Then she begins to curse herself as it was she who started the story of 'no peace.' Despite being in possession of the better combination of head and body, she still feels like a loser. "It is my fault, I mixed the heads up and I must suffer for it" (129) As about Karnad, Suman Bala in her article 'This Mad Dance of Madness: Search for Completeness' says, "In *Hayavadana* he is seized with the theme of incompleteness and depicts the protagonist Padmini's yearning for completeness, for perfection."[5] Now she wants to quench her thirst for Kapila only by looking at him: "Until my child wakes up . . . may I sit here and look at you? Have my fill for the rest of my life" (125). Here Bhagavata significantly intervenes: "That's what Padmini must tell Kapila. . . . Kapila if that Rishi had given me to you, would I have gone back to Devadatta like this" (125) and the intended answer appears to be in the affirmative. Devadatta, finding Padmini again with Kapila, feels torn in this tangled relationship. He helplessly asks Kapila, "You call yourself my friend. But you cannot understand me at all." And Kapila quips, "And have you understood me? No, you haven't" (125). Asked by Devadatta if he really still loves Padmini he nods in the positive and asks Devadatta if they all three can live together like Pandavas and Draupadi. Devadatta declines and proposes, "What won't end has to be cut" (129) pointing at the sword he has got with him.

Then they kill each other and no body knows whether it is suicide or murder. Padmini remains only the onlooker and feels cheated once more. She does not know who her actual husband is: the figure with Devadatta's body or the figure with Devadatta's head; and for whom should she perform Sati. Her death is the last resort to escape the tangled relationships which she fails to comprehend in her lifetime. It is from this angle only that the theme of the play is viewed as complex one by a critic as he says: "Karnad good-humouredly yet critically manipulates the very concepts of the rational and the physical. The multiplicity of the characters and their individual psychic circles playing into each other build up a complex pattern of human relationships. And by projecting these human sympathies against a gradually intensifying clash of personalities, Karnad presents a comprehensive picture of the human beings."

Idea of Love and Sexuality

Feeling of Love and Sexuality is also a common theme in the plays of Girish Karnad. As he always builds up his thought against the background of Indian tradition, his attitude towards love and sex is also compatible. In the Hindu mythology the sexual feeling, which is called Kama, has been awarded special importance like Eros of the Greek and Cupid of the Latins. 'Kama' is the Hindu God of Love and is the son of Brahma. It enjoys everlasting youth and is believed to be the most handsome of all gods. In the *Rig Veda* Kama (literally meaning desire) is described as the "first movement that arose in the one, after it had come into life through the power of fervour of abstraction." In the Puranas also the god of love or sex appears and his main function is to create sexual desire in men and women. The moment Kama was born he let loose a shaft on his father. Wounded with this shaft, the creator of the universe (Brahma) fell in love with his own daughter. The Hindu scripture describes in detail the mischief done by this god of love in every sphere:

> Kama roams about the woodlands, fountains, cities and villages on errands of love, creates desire in ascetics and causes weakness in various women. Wounded by the shafts of Kama, faithful wives become adulterous, young ladies yield themselves to betrayers and youthful men commit follies. Lean Rishis practising austerities give up asceticism and run after women. Countless indeed are the mischiefs done by the God of love.[4]

This vitality of sex is also illustrated by thinkers like Freud who also maintain that all human activities are governed by the sexual instinct in man. The 'Libido' is the primal source of all liteological energy, feels Freud. He holds that the sexual instinct, Libido, is the most basic instinct in man.

In Karnad's dramatic world too, the mother and son can havc sexual attraction (*Tughlaq*); a king can share bed with his attendant and can make her his queen for his lust (*Yayati*); a woman can love the husband's friend when her husband is physically weak (*Hayavadana*); a woman can conceive from a king cobra when her husband is interested in some other woman (*Nagamandala*) and a married woman willingly offers herself to her old lover after being away from her husband for a long time (*The Fire and the Rain*).

The relationship between the king Yayati and Sharmishtha is that of a king and his pretty attendant. Though Sharmishtha is the old fast friend of Devyani (the present queen of the king), she never claims to be her rival in love. After Yayati has accepted Devyani as his queen, Sharmishtha is resigned to her lot as an attendant. However, she has not forgotten the woman in her:

> Do you think I was always like now. I too had once a scent of youth, I would die for the smell of land that is caused by the first sprinkle of rain. After putting off the candle, I would sit by it waiting fearlessly to see in darkness with the twinkling eyes like that of a cat. I would stroll in trees and plants to see a spider weaving a shiny net in the light of sun. (21)

It shows that she too has a feminine self which has always been in search of the masculine. When she attempts to take poison, Yayati forbids her holding her hand. When she reminds him of the significance of holding the right hand of a woman, he withdraws it at once. But he soon orders his attendant Swaranlata not to let anybody enter his room and "sits by her on the same bed." In the next scene he is found smiling, and Sharmishtha's hair is spread over her shoulders. She sits with him covering her head with her 'sari.' Thus from an attendant, she becomes a queen. After seducing Sharmishtha, Yayati feels young again as he tells Sharmishtha: "If it concerned somebody else, I would have agreed. . . . I have been winning over the hearts of many girls with my talks and handsomeness. But today Sharmishtha has taken me by surprise. . . . If I want to have peace, I will have to win her over. . . . I was feeling old. Sharmishtha has enthused me and returned my youth to me. I cannot leave her" (35).

The relationship between Padmini and Kapila in *Hayavadana* has also sexual connotations, though, no doubt, it remains confined to attraction only. In the beginning the sexual liberty of Padmini is hinted at and it is asserted that love cannot be restricted to a single person: "Why should love stick to the sap of a single body? When the stem is drunk with the thick yearning of the many-petalled, many flowered Lantana, why should it be tied down to the relation of a single flower?" (82). Subsequently, Padmini develops a liking for Kapila because her own husband has a small feminine waist which looks "so helpless." On the other hand, her liking for Kapila explains itself: "What an ethereal shape! Such a broad back—like an ocean with muscles rippling across it. He is like a celestial being reborn as a hunter. . . . How his body sways, his limbs curve—it's a dance almost" (96). Even Devadatta confesses and justifies her attraction towards Kapila in an 'Aside.' He feels that no woman could resist him and it is nothing strange if Padmini likes him despite being married. Rather he curses himself for not understanding her physical desire. He would only blame Kapila for "begging for a favour." But he fails to look in the eyes of Padmini: "Only I see the depths—Now I see these flames leaping up from these depths. Now! . . . Look at these yellow, purple flames. Look now she is pouring her soul in his mould. Look!" (96).

After Padmini has mixed up the heads and bodies, she is curious to go with the body of Kapila, with Devadatta's head. Even before their case is decided by the Rishi she has already made up her mind to go with Devadatta. It is the same body which she used to cherish before this incident. When Kapila (with Devadatta's body) makes his claim over her, she feels angry: "Aren't you ashamed of yourself?" (106) and asks him to "shut up." She calls him "rascal" and "brute." When Kapila points out the shrewdness of Padmini saying, "I know what you want, Padmini Devadatta's clever head and Kapila's strong body," Devadatta calls it natural and finds there is nothing wrong in it: "It's natural for a woman to feel attracted to a fine figure of a man" (108). After the case is decided by the Rishi the first thing Padmini admires is the new Devadatta in his body. She caresses his shoulders and says, "What a wide chest. What other canopy do I need?" (111).To her, he appears like a bridegroom with an ornament of a new body. But the moment they part ways with Kapila, Padmini finds it hard to leave him alone. She tells him not to feel sad but to wait and promises to meet him again. He should "cheer up" himself, feels Padmini, as she is going with his body. Actually, she is cheering up herself as well.

Sexuality in *Nagamandala* is portrayed with the help of a cobra. Rani, the main character, is married to Appanna. Their marriage is not solemnized as there is no physical union between the two. Appanna spends nights with his concubine outside and his wife has to stay alone at night. This separation from her husband sexually tortures her. So she readily follows the solution of Kurudavva, the friend of her mother-in-law. The first thing she does without the knowledge of her husband is that she stealthily meets Kurudavva. Had he not stayed out at night she would never have listened to her advice. She develops intimacy with her in no time as if she were already waiting for someone to come to her rescue. When she explains to him the story of the 'two pieces of a root,' Rani listens to it very attentively. She laughs for the first time after her marriage when Kurudavva narrates how the root given by a mendicant helped her in marrying a man and "it took the plague to detach him from her." Perhaps, she has found a ray of hope in Kurudavva's story. She requests her to come again. She makes the paste of the root and mixes it up in the milk boiled for Appanna. He drinks it, but she fails to win him for her nights. Again when she is locked, "then it rains for seven days and seven nights. It pours. The sea floods the city. The waters break down the door of the castle" (35). It is actually the flood of feminine desire in her for her husband. When Kurudavva further suggests to her to use the larger piece of the root and assures her that Appanna will carry her to his concubine's house, she "blushes" (36).

When Naga visits her on the first night Rani's feminine-self is all joy but she doesn't know how to express it. She simply stands "dazed" leaning against the wall. Confused with joy she asks him for food even at midnight at which Naga laughs. And when he assures her that he will come every night she laughs "shyly." Then she puts her head against his shoulder and he puts his arm around her. Now she falls asleep as she has undergone enough sexual insomnia. During his next visit Naga wants to know whether she likes his night visit or not, Rani becomes emotional: "(*Eyes filling up*) Why do you tease me like this? I am sick of being alone. . . . I was desperate that you should come again tonight" (42). The modest Rani becomes unable to hide her feminine desires for too long.

After the physical union between Naga and Rani, we find Rani hiding her face behind her knees and arms wrapped around her legs. No doubt, the first sexual experience shakes her but it also infuses new courage in her and turns out to be a turning point in her life. For the first time the docile Rani gathers courage to acquire a confident tone: "Go away! Don't talk to me" and warns Naga not to say anything against her parents. Naga tries to pacify her by explaining to her that sex is the most basic instinct in everyone and he is no exception. The universality of this sexual instinct in every living creature is put by him thus:

> The female begins to smell like the wet earth. And stung up by her smell, the king cobra starts searching for his queen! The tiger bellows for his mate. When the flame of the forest blossoms into a fountain of red and earth cracks at the touch of the serial roots of the banyan, it moves in the hollow of the cottonwood, in the flow of the estuary, the dark limestone caves from the womb of the heavens to the dark netherworlds, within everything that sprouts, grows, stretches, creaks and blooms—everywhere, those who come together cling, fail apart lazily! It is there and there and there, everywhere. (49)

It cools down Rani and thereafter, she never likes to part with him. She runs to him and embraces him before he goes out. She curses the birds that show by their chirping that the night is over and they should depart now: "Why don't those birds choke on their own songs? Who has given them the right to mess about with other creatures' night?" (45) And when Kurudavva inquires if she has started her married life, "she blushes" and then "laughs." Perhaps she wants to laugh aloud but she doesn't. Then she asks Kurudavva to come again. From this it is evident that the physical union with Naga has actually delighted her.

Rani has ample proof that the person who visits her at night is not actually her husband. But why she should be suspicious and spoil her nights when her husband does not satisfy her physically and emotionally. Whenever there is doubt about Naga's identity, she has no desire to confirm it. She seems to suspend her disbelief willingly. When looking for an ointment for the wounds of Naga she opens up the mirror-box and in the mirror finds a cobra in place of Appanna, she does not confirm it by just looking into the mirror again. Moreover, Naga disappears from the room when her door is locked from outside, and, Kurudavva too tells her that they have seen a cobra coming out of the bathroom drain and no human being has come out. Even, in the morning she finds no scar on the face of Appanna. He too says the dead dog was not an ordinary hound and it has cornered a cheetah once. He asks, "It must have sensed the cobra. It must have given a fight. Didn't you hear at night?" (48) and she shakes her head for 'no.' Here, she deliberately applies no brain of hers. Furthermore, after the fight with a mongoose, Naga stops visiting her. In the morning, she sees the bits of snake-skin in the mongoose teeth but she does not doubt it either. Naga does not turn up for fifteen days and she misses him very much. When he reappears his body is covered with partly healed wounds. Again she applies ointment and nurses his wounds but she never questions him about it. Perhaps she does not want to lose him again, "it was enough that he had returned" (49). The Appanna during the day and the Appanna at night have major noticeable differences especially of wounds on their faces, but Rani never gives serious thought to it. She simply forgets everything when the thought of Naga and the nights with him occurs to her mind: "There it is . . . the smell of the blossoming night queen! How it fills the house before he comes. How it welcomes him! God, how it takes me, sets each fibre in me on fire" (49). She waits throughout the day to burn with this fire at night. Her joy knows no bounds when she is to inform her 'night-husband' that she is pregnant—her doubt that her nights are only a dream has turned into a reality: "I was a stupid, ignorant girl, when you brought me here. But now a woman, a wife and I am going to be mother. I am not a parrot. Not a cat or sparrow" (50) as she has always been treated at day time. It is only Naga that cures her of frigidity with affection, patience and tact. Naga here functions as a "male sex surrogate"[9] in curing Rani of frigidity. Rani says that she is not scared of anything, if anything scares her that is the thought of losing her night-life which she wishes to lose at no cost:

"I don't want any tomorrows or days after. I want night to last forever. . . . I mustn't let you go. I must listen to my heart and hold you back. Take you like a baby in my arms and make you safe" (55). The mother in Rani consoles Naga "like a baby." First she used to behave as a baby in the presence of Appanna. It is with the love of Naga that she grows up. She would behave "as a frightened child in the presence of Appanna. She grows as she receives the affection of Naga. She, a little helpless indifferent girl, gradually becomes a confident and courageous lady."

Love and sex remain the point of concern in man-woman relationships cutting across social, religious, and caste lines in *The Fire and the Rain*. The first love story presented before us is through Arvasu and Nittilai. Both are in their teens: Arvasu is nineteen years old and Nittilai is just fourteen. Their teenage love is in progress and they are planning to get married. If Rani in *Nagamandala* is to face the Elders of Appanna's village for having sexual relations with a man other than her husband, Arvasu is to face the Elders of Nittilai's tribe. It is their tribal custom that every young man in order to marry their daughter has to appear before the Elders first. But here things are rather complex as Arvasu is a Brahmin and Nittilai is a hunter girl. Their orthodox family won't allow this inter-caste marriage. Arvasu respects his elder brother Paravasu, a rigid Brahmin, but won't sacrifice his love for Nittilai for his sake. He is ready to face the Elders but because he could not reach there in time, he is refused Nittilai's hand. Her brother knocks her down and plants his foot on his chest as he feels he has caused them a trouble and is humiliating them by calling their sister's name in public. But they fail to check the lovers meeting each other in private. Nittilai runs away from her husband and comes to stay with Arvasu. Hearing about her lover's miseries inflicted by her parents and by his own brother, she rushes for Arvasu's help.

Being a hunter woman she does not have sexual relation with Arvasu before or after her marriage. But the intensity of her love for Arvasu is beyond any doubt. The risk of her life fails to check her meeting him. She loves him very much and it is because of this relationship that she has interest in her life too: "Do you think I want to die? You think I want to be hunted down by my brother and my husband? . . . Arvasu. I am still young. I don't want to die" (40). But when Arvasu runs amuck playing the role of Vritra she rushes to his help and tragically her throat is slashed by her husband. Thus only death separates the two lovers from each other.

Vishakha is another character in *The Fire and the Rain* who unlike Nittilai asserts her sexuality in her own way. She has had a romantic encounter with Yavakri before her marriage. Ten years ago when her lover came to bid her good bye as he was to leave for the forest life, she lost control over herself. Succumbing to her bodily desires she led him quickly to the jack-fruit grove behind her house. She "opened the knot of her blouse and pressing my face to your breasts, and turned and fled" (17), remembers Yavakri. No doubt, time has affected her body as her, "Breasts hang now," feels she, but her urge to be loved is young as ever. She hints at her unsatisfied sexual urges time and again when she meets Yavakri for the second time.

If Rani willingly suspends her disbelief about the identity of Naga because her husband does not satisfy her sexually, Vishakha willingly offers herself to Yavakri on his second visit to her. Even having been married, she fails to resist much on seeing him after a long time. She sits down and readily agrees to listen to him. The moment he tries to kiss her she loses control over herself. Admitting that Yavakri has rekindled "her desire to talk," she says, "I thought it was dead and gone. Gently, don't rush . . . and words are like water—precious. I was afraid to bathe. Now I want to drown" (16). Vishakha has been left alone by her husband for a long time. She feels very much delighted in giving catharsis to her pent-up feelings by narrating her sexual experience to her old lover. She makes frank confession about the fact that the married life of one year gave her a great joy as her husband plunged her into a kind of bliss. She didn't know that she even existed: it was a "heaven for her." Then on the first day of the second year of her marriage they started for their search as she narrates the experience of her erotic pleasure: "He plunged me into a kind of bliss I didn't know existed. It was heaven—here and now—at the tip of all my senses. Then . . . he used my body, and his own body like an experimenter, an explorer. As instruments in a search. Search for what? I never knew. . . . Nothing was too shameful, too degrading, even too painful. Shame died in me. And I yielded. I let my body be turned inside out as he did his own. I had a sense he was leading me to something. Mystical? Spiritual? We never talked. Only the sense pervaded the air" (16).

Her sharing of this erotic experience with Yavakri tells a lot about her suppressed sexuality. Perhaps she longs to repeat the experience somehow; she also reveals how neither her husband nor her lover could take cognizance of her feminine self. Significantly she divulges, "I shall give you the knowledge Indra could not give you—my body" (17).

About her meeting with Yavakri, Vishakha makes no pretence when her husband inquires about it. She is not ashamed of anything, "whatever you heard about Yavakri and me . . . was no rumour" (31). She honestly confesses that he and Yavakri have much resemblance with each other. She justifies her husband's secret visit to her at night: "I suppose that would be too human. But what's wrong with being human? What's wrong with being happy?" (32) She also praises Yavakri in her husband's presence as Padmini praises Kapila in Devadatta's presence. She says "At least Yavakri was warm, gentle." Finally, her desire to be killed by her husband may be taken as a last resort on her part to escape the sexual suffering she has been undergoing.

Contemporary India in Traditional Material

The most formidable aspect of Karnad's modernity lies in his picturization of contemporary Indian political, social and religious scene. From the viewpoint of contemporary Indian scene *Tughlaq* and *Tale-Danda* are very important. If *Tughlaq* deals with a historical figure in the history of India, *Tale-Danda* deals with a regional incident that took place in Karnataka. The two plays not only refer to the historical past but also to the current Indian scene in respect to the political and socio-cultural reality.

First of all in Muhammad we find a modern Indian ruler who has opportunistic views about religion. He believes and disbelieves in God as the situation demands. He uses religion for his political ends only. Muhammad's hypocrisy and arrogance and the resultant suffering of his subjects depict the present Indian scene.

The first scene that opens in front of the Chief Court of Justice in Delhi, reminds us of the present-day India with a mixture of Hindus and Muslims. Then the opening sentence of the play, "God, what's this country coming to?" reflects the present scenario where every Indian who is generally religious and has faith in its rich cultural heritage seems to ask. The drift of the present-day India from its past is a matter of concern for every one. This sentence suggests the widening gap between what India and Indianness was and what it has been reduced to by its rulers. The Indians hated the Britishers and pushed them out because they deprived the Indians of their rights, exploited them, deceived them and finally made them strangers in their own land. But independence, too, brought no substantial change for the common Indian. Rather, the situation deteriorated from bad to worse; the common Indian is being deceived by his own countrymen and there is complete degeneration of human values. The feeling of brotherhood and commonness which stood its ground in the face of foreigners' rule began to vanish soon after independence. So the old man's concern for 'what the country is coming to?' becomes so relevant in this context. His lament is the lament of every Indian when human values have taken a back seat; "I don't know.

I've been alive a long time, seen many Sultans, but I never thought I would live to see a thing like this." (147).

Muhammad's hypocritical attitude towards religion and the religious practices is also identical to the attitude of political leaders of independent India. They use religion for their political motives. In the opening scene of the play the young man defends Muhammad as he is a staunch believer in Islam, saying: "Tell me, how often did you pray before he came to the throne? . . . Not even once a week, I bet. Now you pray five times a day because that's the law and if you break it, you'll have the officers at your neck. Can you mention one earlier Sultan in whose time people read the Koran in the streets like now?" (147) At this the old man rightly points out the futility of such an exercise: "What's the use? One must act according to it." This indeed is a hint at the mask of religion the Indian rulers are wearing and the meaninglessness of their religious slogans.

The communal crack in the Hindus and the Muslims during Muhammad's regime also speaks of the communal atmosphere of the present-day India. 'The Third Man' is critical about the Hindus who are not paying the Jaziya tax which he feels is against the Koran. The all-pervasive nature of Hinduism with which it has absorbed many other small religions is also referred to by the old man. He says, "Beware of the Hindu who embraces you. Before you know that, he will turn Islam into another caste and call the Prophet an incarnation of his god" (148). This reflects the inherent fear of Muslims as a minority community. They nurse a feeling that their community can be taken into its fold by Hinduism. And the final reference to the communal riots in Kanpur is highly suggestive of the current communal violence in various parts of India.

Muhammad, outwardly benevolent but inwardly deceptive, is like the present Indian ruler who carries deep-rooted duality in his character. Muhammad says, "My beloved people, you have . . . seen how justice works in my kingdom without any consideration of might or weakness of religion or creed" (149). The modern Indian leader similarly plays with the religious feelings of the people. Muhammad's attempt to look a true Muslim king by making prayer five times a must in one day is basically a political device. In fact, he has murdered his own father in prayer and announced that it was an accident. His inner self is that of an atheist. The non-believer in him has put the Sayyids and the Ulema behind the bars but to the public he announces, "I've never denied the word of God. Because it is my bread and my drink" (164). He has Muslims, Hindus and Jains etc. in his country, so he speaks the language which offends none. His approach to religion is purely political. Like an Indian ruler he has no hesitation to proclaim, "I have never denied the word of God. . . . Because it is my bread and butter. . . . Only an atheist can try to be God. I am God's most humble slave." After an attempt is made on his life, he bans prayer forever only to revoke the ban later. Thus the idea of prayer in the play becomes an image of the idea of religion in general which is used and misused by the rulers for their convenience. Iman-ud-din's advice to Muhammad is very apt, "Religion! Politics! take heed, one day these verbal distinctions will rip you into two" (165). This is how politics is deftly linked with religion in this play. Using religion for politics, Muhammad compels Sheikh Iman-ud-Din to be his envoy and kills him without a little mercy. The Sheikh rightly views, "I am just going to understand why they say you are the cleverest man in the world."

Muhammad's dreams of the future are identical with the dreams of Independent India. U.R. Anantamurthy observes, "It is a play of the Sixties and reflects as perhaps no other play does the political mood of disillusionment which followed the Nehru era of idealism in the country." Muhammad too wants to "build an ideal empire" (149). His new steps of shifting the capital from Delhi to Daulatabad and change the currency remind of the new experiments introduced in independent India. The socio-economic measures in the form of Five Year Plans, the introduction of democracy through newly framed constitution and many more new national and international policies formulated by the rulers of independent India and the inherent contradictions in them carry implicit comment of the playwright. By showing the result of the innovative experiments made by Muhammad, Karnad appears to be apprehensive about the policies and their implementation in independent India. Muhammad's idealism appears to have a close parallel in the mood of disillusionment which followed Nehru era of idealism in the country. In the words of Girish Karnad, "In a sense, the play reflected this slow disillusionment of my generation felt with the new politics of independent India: the gradual erosion of the ethical norms that had guided the movement of independence, and coming to terms with cynicism and realpolitik."

However, Karnad denies having made any conscious effort to associate the rule of Muhammad Tughlaq with that of Nehru. He feels that the similarity between the two is "accidental," as he says, "I did not consciously write about the Nehru era. I am always flattered when people tell me that it was about the Nehru era. But, I think, well, that it is a compliment that any playwright would be thrilled to get, but it was not intended to be a contemporary play about a contemporary situation."

The atmosphere of violence, bloodshed, treachery and corruption from top to the bottom in *Tughlaq* is suggestive of the contemporary Indian socio-political scene. The people of independent India have confronted two major problems: poverty and violence generated by the wrong political policies. If Muhammad's subjects rush from Delhi to Daulatabad with high hopes then the people of India too had high hopes when they shifted from British rule to self-rule. Like them the Indians too met with disappointment and frustration in place of peace and prosperity. Instead of gaining anything, they experience corruption and disorderliness all around. About the contemporary relevance of the play, Tejwant S. Gill aptly remarks, "No wonder, the life, rule and time of this charismatic and erratic emperor have past significance, the present meaning . . . is getting more and more pronounced with the passage of time."[5]

Mixing up of caste and religion with politics remains a dominant idea in *Tale-Danda*. The caste system which finds only a casual reference in the first play *Yayati* and then *Tughlaq* becomes a major issue in *Tale-Danda*: A.R. Shukla says: "The central theme of *Tale-Danda* is that of deconstruction of caste and religion to arrive at its real, proper meaning and to restructuring the same for the benefit of the society and the country." Now the playwright is in the mood to launch a campaign against the division of society on the basis of caste. As according to the rigid Hindu tradition: "There are four Varnas: Brahmins, Kshatriyas, Vaishyas and Shudras. Their functions are priesthood and education, administration and war, trade and production work. Brahmins are the most privileged of all and the last class which is not considered a Varna is that of untouchables."[6]

Thus a man in the traditional Hindu society is not recognized by his worth but by his caste. To quote Manu who categorizes human society on inhuman grounds and puts the Brahmin caste at the top of the caste hierarchy, "Thus whatsoever exists in the universe is all the property of the Brahmins; for the Brahmin is entitled to it all by his superiority and eminence of birth." He further says: "But a Shudra (whether bought or not bought), the Brahmins may compel to practice servitude, for that (Shudra) was created by the self existent merely for the service of the Brahmins. Even if freed by his master, the Shudra is not released from servitude, for this [servitude] is innate in him, who then can take it from him?"[7]

In other words, a Shudra is not considered a human being and so he is even prohibited to read Vedas. This practice has not changed the Indian mind since ages and *Tale-Danda* exposes this ugly deformity of the Hindu society. In this play the movement against this social evil is launched by the Sharanas. For them, sincerity of action and selfless service of humanity is a true religion in which all human beings are equal. But the king Bijjala in the play accepts this new religion only to the extent it serves his political interests. In spite of being a Shudra by caste he does not support inter-caste marriage as he perceives strong objections from the upper caste people. His attitude to caste system is confined to his power-politics only.

Bijjala, in his conversation with his wife Rambhavati, appreciates the cause of the Sharanas. He knows that they want to eradicate the caste-system "from the face of the earth. Annihilate the Varna system, what a vision! And what prodigious courage!" (15). But when his wife questions him why doesn't he join them too, his answer is "It'll solve nothing." Quoting the verse of Basavanna, he tells his wife that "It is not, as you can see, an ethics designed for rulers, worse still in their 'Bhakti' their devotion, their incessant craving for the Lord's grace" (15). Here we remember the duality in Muhammad's character as a king. Like him, Bijjala also feels that a ruler has different ethics to follow. Bijjala too has built temples, but with a political aim. He frankly says, "I've built temples to keep my subjects happy. But the one truth I know is that I exist and God doesn't" (15). He says that he is an ordinary king and he wants "No truck with the gods. I go by the laws of the land, which is why this mass hunger for divine grace bothers me greatly" (23). But he never keeps religion and politics apart and recognizes that Basavanna like Imam-ud-Din in *Tughlaq* has sway over the masses as a religious leader. So he sends Basavanna to Maddu to pacify his violent followers.

Bijjala and Basavanna's relationship, like that of Muhammad and Sheikh Imam-ud-Din, can also be interpreted in modern political sense where religious and social heads are patronized by the rulers for their political gains. Muhammad uses Sheikh for his political purpose. Likewise, Bijjala's attitude towards Basavanna is purely politics-oriented. He likes his philosophy so far as it enhances his own interest as a king. But he would not let it grow beyond a limit. He brings Basavanna and his followers to his territory as they are only to earn the day's keep, make no extra demand and treat profits with contempt. This attitude helps only the king. He confesses, "For their honest labour, trade and commerce have come pouring into Kalyan and now the city is bursting with money. Even those who despise the Sharanas for their beliefs need them for their economic enterprise—as indeed I do" (24). So his direct and indirect support to the Sharanas is not without politics in it. He allows them some liberty not because their cause is just but because he needs them.

About the contemporaneity in *Tale-Danda* Karnad in his interview in *Frontline* observed, "When people all-around us are slaughtered in the name of the temple, I hear echoes from those times long past . . . it seems eight hundred years have solved no problem. We are back exactly where we started." Like the communal violence at Kanpur in Tughlaq, in *Tale-Danda* too, the Jain temples are being occupied by force. The Sharanas threaten to "smash the naked idols and turn it into a Shiva temple" (28). This is a typical incident which reminds us of the communal violence at Ayodhya and the challenge of the orthodox Hindus in India to demolish the mosque of the Muslim community.

In *Tale-Danda* too the fundamentalists won't let the tribals of Andhra and Gangodho enter their territory and their side of the river because the tribals are low-caste. Basavanna appears to be the spokesman of Karnad when he asks other Sharanas to shun violence in any form. Basavanna's remark in response to Jagadeva's idea is relevant to the contemporary Indian scene: "Violence is wrong, whatever the provocation. Who resorts to it because someone else started it first is even worse. And to do so in the name of structure of brick and mortar is a monument of stupidity" (29). The words of Basavanna reflect the modern Indian socio-political crisis and provide the answer as well:

The rich

Will make temple of Shiva
What shall I
A poor man do?
My legs are pillars
The body, the shrine
The head of cupola
Of gold. . . .
Things standing shall fall
But the moving shall ever stay. (29)

These words of Basavanna appear to hint at the root cause of all communal problems in India, i.e., we are stagnant in thinking and we should widen our visions. About the so-called miracles, which the Indians are more prone to believe in, he says, "Isn't this life abundant enough? Do we need more miracles?" (29)

The current idea of religious conversion from one religion to another can also be derived from the happenings in *Tale-Danda*. Kalyana and Gundanna inform Basavanna about the arrival of some tribals in the region. Kalyana suggests to Basavanna about their belief in idol worship and desires that they should be taken in the Sharanas' fold: "Basavanna, those tribes have brought their god with them. You should see that idol. Rolling eyes, a tongue rolling out. . . . So the sooner they initiate them into their fold the better" (35). But Basavanna's approach is highly realistic as is evident from his reply, "A roof over their head first and a piece of land to spread their mate on. We can minister to their spiritual needs later." This view is important in the contemporary context where some Hindu organizations are getting seamy as the people from the low castes are converting to Christianity. So our priority, as per the message of the play, should be to address the physical needs of the people and the spiritual concern should be secondary at present. Gangambhika, the wife of Basavanna, is offering bags of paddy, textiles, salt and spices for the tribals who are coming from Andhra. The sufferings of these tribes who have tracked for weeks in search of food and shelter, and, hunger and starvation of the people on their way from Delhi and Daulatabad in Tughlaq, remind us of the poverty in India. Chaman Ahuja rightly observes, "his works make telling comments on the general human situation and the specific socio-political goings on in the country today."

As a modern playwright, Girish Karnad has a feeling of revolt against the established orthodoxy. Herbert Read in the foreword to *The Rebel* quotes Albert Camus:

> Revolt is one of the 'essential dimensions' of mankind. It is useless to deny its historical reality. Rather we must seek in it a principle of existence. But the nature of revolt has changed radically in our times. It is no longer the revolt of the slaves against the masters, nor even the revolt of the poor against the rich; it is a metaphysical revolt, the revolt of man against the condition of life, against creation itself. At the same time it's an aspiration towards clarity and unity of thought—even paradoxically towards order.[8]

This idea of revolt is prevalent in almost all of Karnad's plays from *Yayati* to *The Fire and the Rain*. His characters tend to rebel against the orthodox religious, social and political order. This modern feeling of discontent which results from his modern outlook is mainly against the so-called social values which are hollow within but tend to restrain man's individuality.

In *Yayati* the revolt is against the man-made social relationships in which we aspire to be superhuman. This revolt is manifested mainly through Chitralekha who is a 'rebel' in Camus's sense. Camus's rebel is he who says: "this has been going on for too long . . . 'no further,' 'you are going too far' . . . there are certain limits beyond which you shall not go. . . . He rebels because he categorically refuses to submit to the conditions that he considers intolerable. Because in his mind he thinks that he has the right."[9]

Chitralekha too feels that Yayati has gone 'too far' by depriving her husband of his youth. Further, he refuses to own his responsibilities towards her. She does not yield to the commands of Yayati. Pleading his case, Yayati says "Right or wrong . . . leave it, don't feel sad for nothing I have the realization of your situation. . . . All that's gone is over. Now you should behave as the princess of Angkul should do or as the daughter-in-law of Bharatkul should. . . . I promise you Chitralekha, I won't keep Puru's youth for many years. I will give it back after fulfilling my aim" (72).But she remains unmoved by his emotional speech and asserts that she won't let Puru enter Anantpur until he regains his youth. She lashes out at his father-in-law when he likes to treat her as a lifeless thing: "You are the man to push him near his funeral . . . not me; and you are advising me without knowing my grief. You are giving a long speech? The poor, a stupid son you got. Putting all the burden of your sin on his neck, you are advising me for womanliness?" (73-74)

When he urges her to be thoughtful, her rebellious voice becomes rather louder. She expresses her inability to push her original self under the 'cover' of thoughts. She asks him a very practical question, i.e., "Can you imagine what will be his [Puru's] age by the time you complete your aim" (75). When the king replies that he wants to possess Puru's youth for only six years, she is very straightforward in her reaction: "Only six years! Only . . . I don't want your youth. I got this youth just fifteen days ago. It went away trampling my dreams spread over the pillow with its feet. What six years are you talking about?" (75). When Yayati requests her in the name of the future of his people and advises her to sacrifice herself for the sake of the state, she values her present more than the future of Yayati: "But I have taken birth. Your bright future is not born yet. Should I sacrifice my own existence for the sake of a bubble which is yet to be born" (75). And finally she challenges him to accept the other reality, i.e., to accept her as his wife, "So, it is logical that you should not hide behind any reason or logic. . . . You snatched youth from my husband. So it is natural that you should accept everything concerning it" (77). When he tries to silence her in the name of humanity and her loyal background, she becomes more vocal and says that she has lost faith in such ideas. There are no human beings but only "masks," feels Chitralekha. But when she realizes that no logic can defeat Yayati—neither would he accept her nor would he give back her husband's youth—she takes poison. She declines to follow his way of life that wears the mask of morality. She expresses her inability to play the game suggested by Yayati. Caught in a strange dilemma, in which neither can she enjoy the youth of her husband nor can she embrace Yayati's philosophy of self-denial, she prefers death like Padmini in *Hayavadana*. But before her death she makes Yayati realize that she is right and Yayati and his son both are wrong. After her death the defeated Yayati calls Puru and says, "I have a request. Take my youth back" (82). Therein lies the victory of Chitralekha. The final recognition of the horror draws upon Yayati through Chitralekha. Her suicide brings him to awareness and he owns up the responsibility for his actions. "The fear of sacrifice led me to sexual pleasure but this unnatural youth could not obtain that. Puru, take back your youth. . . . There could be no better lesson than Chitralekha's death" (22).

Existentialistic Idea of Revolt

In *Hayavadana* this revolt is posed by Padmini. She revolts against the traditional idea that a woman can't love anybody else other than her husband after marriage. She marries Devadatta by choice. But after coming in contact with Kapila she finds a better husband in him. Unlike an Indian wife, she can praise another man in the presence of her husband. She was never a shy woman even on her wedding night. Unlike Devadatta and Kapila she refuses to play the role others expect her to play. When Devadatta dislikes Kapila's frequent visits to their place, Padmini strongly defends Kapila: "Don't blame him. It is my fault. . . . So I asked him to come. . . . He didn't want to. . . . But I insisted" (91). Then she compares the two friends and hints that Kapila is better. In the scene at the temple of Kali when Padmini mixes wrong heads on bodies, Kapila with Devadatta's body shows his claim over her. She won't listen to him now because she has got the combination of her choice in the new Devadatta. She is critical of the absurd human condition and poses a question to the goddess Kali. Getting ready for the Sati in the forest with Kapila she says, "Kali, Mother of all nature, you must have your joke even now. Other women can die praying that they should get the same husband in all the lives to come. You haven't left me even with that little consolation" (131). Thus even in her death, she has the tone of revolt and challenge.

A critic has similar views about the role of Padmini: "Probably what Karnad tries to reveal through Padmini is the predicament of a modern, free and bold woman who is torn between polarities, a woman who loves her husband as well as someone else for two different aspects of their personalities.[24] Commenting on his decision Subhangi S. Raykar views:

> One must choose one's course of action and then accept the consequence unflinchingly. But if understood as a deliberately chosen one Padmini's act is ultimately a consequence of the social norms imposed on her. Since she cannot have both Devadatta and Kapila she tries to get past the norms by having what she most wants from each of them.

Her voice of challenge and revolt touches a new height when she returns to Kapila again leaving her husband behind for the second time.

Rani in *Nagamandala* does not stand for this type of revolt. She is not vocal and authoritative like Padmini: her challenge is implicit. She suffers meekly at the hands of her cruel husband and remains silent throughout her suffering. She not only spends nights with Naga but is indifferent to the reality about it. Maybe she cannot gather enough courage to question why the Appanna during day time is different from the Appanna at night. Even in her chastity-test, she does not tell a lie. She says that she has touched only "two" in her life. She could say that she had touched only her husband but using the word 'two' she asserts herself. When she learns about the death of the cobra she feels sad, "Oh poor thing, it is dead!" (63). She feels that their son has been given the gift of life by the cobra "as by a father." Hence, she instructs her husband that the cobra has to be ritually cremated. Moreover, "when we cremate this snake, the fire should be lit by our son. . . . And every year on this day, our son should perform the rituals to commemorate its death" (63). Appanna questions the validity of this ritual as he feels that she is going too far. When he questions her strange behaviour towards the cobra as he himself is still alive, Rani retorts, "Please don't say no" (63). When Appanna is away, her eyes fill with tears at the death of cobra. She bows down to it and picking it up presses it to her cheeks. In the second ending of the play, she protects the cobra, her love, from her husband and there lies the challenge to the traditional bond between husband and wife where wife is not supposed to conceal anything from her husband. She guides the cobra:

> What are you doing here? He'll kill you. Go. Go away. No! Not that way. He's here. What shall we do? Why did you ever come in here stupid? (Suddenly) My hair? Of course, come, quickly climb into it! (She lets her hair down to the floor). Quick now. Get in. Are you safely in there? Good now stay there. And like still . . . This hair is symbol of my wedded bliss. Live there happily, forever. (54).

For the sake of her old love she tells a lie to her husband. Because of this implicit challenge in Rani's behaviour the play is sometimes called a feminist play. The character of Rani interrogates the patriarchal moral code which demands the faithfulness of woman to her husband but not the faithfulness of man to his wife.

The revolt in *Tale-Danda* is shown through Basavanna, his followers and Bijjala as well. Bijjala, the king, is not from any higher caste. He is a barber and still he is full of kingly insight. He realizes that to be a king heredity is no qualification. He rejects Sovideva as his descendent as he lacks the qualities of a ruler. He is in complete agreement with Basavanna when he opines, "Kingship is a calling. A source of living, yes, but also a duty and a service of humanity. It is not an inheritance, not a family gift but a right to be earned, to be justified by diligent application" (20). And Bijjala as a king proves that good administration is not a property only limited to the higher castes. As a king he knows well what he is to do and what not. He likes Sharanas because they are selfless workers but does not fully encourage them because they can be a threat to his throne. When Basavanna offers to step down as his treasurer the king in Bijjala becomes more authoritative, "If you think I have ascended the throne merely to sit back and scratch my arm you are in for surprise—You think you can twist my arms behind my back and push me around—I am Bijjala" (40). Having discovered that his threat trick has not worked and Basavanna is not to budge an inch from his stand, he prefers to withdraw, "So be it. Have your wedding. I won't come in the way because I know I can't" (50). Thus, through Basavanna's definition of kingship and Bijjala's capability as a king, the playwright throws a challenge to the contemporary Indian caste-ridden society.

Even a barber can be an intelligent king, proves the playwright. Basavanna represents change through peaceful and rational means. He uses every logic and rationality to counter the challenge against him. When Bijjala warns him of the violence which the inter-caste marriage is to result in Basavanna's question is very much logical: "But who is being punished for whose crime? Are the birds to be penalized because snakes resent their ability to fly" (48). Thus, we find that Basavanna is determined to go with his peaceful revolt against the orthodox set-up of society but at the same time he is not unaware of the initial hurdles in his way to success. He knows that it will be a terrible blow at the roots of the rigid caste-system as "Bigotry has not faced such a challenge in two thousand years" (38). He is fully aware that if inter-caste marriage takes place, it will generate violence. He suggests to the Sharanas to be very cautious as "It is a question of life and death for these children. From tomorrow, the wrath of the bigoted will pursue them like a swarm of snakes, to strike as they pause to put up a roof or light an oven. Who will protect them then?" (38-39). At the same time, he is not pessimist about the future of the casteless vision of society. He is sure that "Every person will see himself only as a human being. That is inevitable. But we have a long way to go. You know the most terrible sins have been justified in the name of Sanatana religion" (39). When Madhuvarsa says that she is ready to sacrifice her own daughter to forward the cause of the movement, Basavanna is very clear about his mission as he says that none has a right to sacrifice anyone, not even himself. At this Haralayya supports him saying that already many women have been sacrificed to the greed of the upper class and their sons have been sacrificed at the altar of the comic theories of rebirth. It is from this view that Basavanna feels "tardy" to bless the couple though he has immense joy at the growing success of the Sharanas' ideology. His head "trembles" as he feels that the Sharanas are not yet ready for the kind of revolution this wedding is heading for. At this Basavanna's followers accuse him of cowardice. They fear that the Sharanas would become the laughing stock of the world. But Basavanna is more concerned with the well-being and the actions of the Sharanas and is least bothered about what the onlookers say. To Bijjala, however, he makes it clear that marriage will take place at any cost and it does take place. The success of the inter-caste marriage is actually a challenge posed by Basavanna and his followers and Bijjala rightly calls it a miracle: "A Brahmin girl chooses to marry an untouchable and the hundred thousand people come out in support of it. That is the only miracle Basavanna has ever performed" (65). In this way, "Karnad revisits history not only to question the notion that Hinduism is a benevolent, monolithic, cultural unity, but also to disprove that religious intolerance is a problem created by modern secularism."[26] Perhaps the playwright gives a hint to the modern Indian ruler who is ignoring the harsh reality about communalism in India. At the same time he provides us the clue about the end of the opportunist rulers through the end of Bijjala. In the preface to the play he says:

> I wrote *Tale-Danda* in 1989 when the Mandir and the Mandal movements were beginning to show how relevant the question posed by these thinkers was for our age. The horror of subsequent events and the religious fanaticism that has gripped our national life today have only proved how dangerous it is to ignore the solutions they offered.

It is from this angle only that a critic observes, "*Tale-Danda* is relevant today as religious fundamentalism is strong enough to destroy the Babri Masjid and claim the lives of thousands of people."[10]

The revolt in *The Fire and the Rain* is presented in more than one way: if Nittilai and Vishakha revolt against the rigidity of society with regard to love, marriage and sex, Arvasu along with his theatre-party presents a revolt against the religious rituals like propitiating gods through worships and sacrifice. Arvasu appears as an excommunicated lover and finishes as the favourite of Lord Indra. Arvasu, in conversation with Andhaka, in Act One, makes clear his uncompromising nature. He is least bothered at his excommunication by his elder brother Paravasu and sticks to what he himself feels as an individual. He does not like to initiate anyone: "I'll never be learned like father or uncle. I shan't even conduct the royal sacrifice like Paravasu or perform penance like cousin Yavakri. All I want is to dance and sing and act. And be with Nittilai" (7). He would rather be an outcaste but he does not like to follow the traditional beaten ways of human society. He has his own way to follow. When he is to appear before the village-elders for marrying Nittilai, he gets late only trying to save the life of Yavakri. Thus he loses the opportunity of marrying his love. He explains it to Nittilai's brother, "How could I leave the dead body with him there and come away?" (26), but none listens to him. Even Arvasu is ready to offer chunks of his flesh to their gods as a penance, he is still beaten up by Nittilai's brother. Arvasu has serious grudge against the people around him and so he desires to avenge himself upon them: "I want to make them all pay. Yavakri. Father. Parvasu. It's conspiracy . . . it is all planned—because I wanted to marry you. Because I was ready to reject my caste, my birth" (43). But Nittilai asks him not to be revengeful. In her passive resistance she stands by Arvasu in raising the banner of revolt: "Then kick that world aside . . . we don't need the world. We can find our own" (44). It is only for this resistance against the rigid ways of society that her head is slashed by her own husband at the end.

If the success of inter-caste marriage in *Tale-Danda* poses a revolt against the caste-ridden Indian society, the success of Arvasu as an actor in *The Fire and the Rain* in bringing about rain by pleasing Lord Indra is another revolt against the superficial religious rituals. In his write up on Girish Karnad Saroj Vasishth remarks:

> *Agni Aur Barkha* is based on two tales from the *Mahabharata* and is a strong forward attack on Brahminical super power. There is a drought and naturally there is a Yajna—a formal rite. The seven-year long structure of this ritual demolishes the very life force within its structure and it rains. . . . Girish Karnad presented Brahmins as the pollutants. For them, Arvasu is the one polluted. It is this very outcaste Arvasu who brings the rain and not the caste Brahmins.

It is significant that the acting of Arvasu and the humanity of Nittilai is juxtaposed with seven years' fire sacrifice by Indra: "We loved the way you challenged Indra and then pursued him. . . . But it could also be because of Parvasu's sacrifice or Nittilai's humanity. . . . The point is we are here and you can ask for anything you want" (39): here lies the victory of Arvasu and Nittilai. In asking Lord Indra for the release of Brahmin Rakshasas' soul, Arvasu takes one more step forward. In fact he revolts against both: the physical and the metaphysical world.

It is interesting to note that the mythic as well as the factual events of the past pass commentary over the contemporary reality. The playwright's immense interest in his past, which is loaded with mythology, is there because it remains an integral part of the living culture in India. The deities of the Indian pantheon are part and parcel of the day-to-day life of the people. Because of their long association with the deities, the supernatural world is more a fact than fiction. Hence, living in the age of reason and science, Karnad doesn't lose touch with tradition, mythology and history which remain a repository of ideas for him.

Karnad does invite criticism from certain quarters for not inventing new plots for his plays. Without making any pretence he confesses:

> Maybe I cannot invent plots. I go in for stories that are exciting, I think these are better stories than I will be able to botch up. At least in this want of originality, I am perhaps as good, or as bad, as Shakespeare. . . . One thing more, I turn not only to myths, legends and history, but also to folklore. In fact, what attracts me most is the archetypal folk tale; with no fact already there. I find in it all the scope for flirting with ideas. I find the great advantage of being able to subvert the traditional, even classical beliefs. Since folk tales make fun of everybody—rulers, priests, even gods, every thing is taken in good humour.

Thus each play gives a different glimpse of Karnad's modern sensibility. His journey from *Yayati* to *The Fire and the Rain*, proves him rather a stern believer in the human spirit. Using folk as mere aesthetic device does not attract him. His faith in man and the reality of his flesh and blood is upheld by each play. His voice of revolt gets sharper and this is how *The Fire and the Rain* dares to shift its focus to the criticism of religious practices like *Yajna* and the world of gods stands more exposed than ever. The mythical tales taken from the *Mahabharata* and the *Ramayana* lose their sanctity and start upholding the scientific modern convictions.

NOTES

1. Seetakant Mahapatra, "The *Mahabharata* and its Relevance to our Times," *The Role of Tradition in Literature* (Delhi: Vikas, 1997), p.3.
2. M.K. Naik, *A History of Indian English Literature* (New Delhi: Sri Saraswati Press, 1982), p.20.
3. Veena Noble Das, "Search for Tradition in Kannada Drama: The Plays of Girish Karnad," *Modern Indian Drama in English Translation* (Hyderabad: Taurus Printers, 1988), p.140.
4. Qtd. P. Thomas, "Love and Sex," *Epics, Myths and Legends of India* (Bombay: Taraporewala, 1952), p.105.
5. Tejwant S. Gill, "*Tughlaq*: Its Past Significance and Present Meaning," *Bharati Journal of Comparative Literature*, Vol. II, No.1 (1987): 57-58.
6. Baba Sahib Ambedkar: *Writings and Speeches* (Bombay: Government of Maharashtra, 1987), p.69.
7. *The Ordinances of Manu,* trans. Edward W. Hopkins (New Delhi: Munshiram Manoharlal, 1971), p.13.
8. Albert Camus. *The Rebel,* trans. Anthony Bower (London, Penguin, 1962), p.7.
9. *Ibid.*, p.19
10. Aparna Dharwadkar, "Playwright and Criticism: Another look at Girish Karnad," *Theatre India*, No.1, May 1999, 83-84.

Tension

Tension is an inherent feature of drama and Girish Karnad's plays are no exception. As a playwright Karnad is always hanging between two forces: the tussle is between two polarities and he seems to be struggling between them. R.K. Dhawan attributes the reason of this tension to the "diverse influences" Karnad went through during his formative years: "He was exposed to a literary scene where there was a direct clash between Western and native tradition. It was India of the Fifties and the Sixties that surfaced two streams of thoughts in all walks of life—adoption of new modernistic techniques, a legacy of the colonial rule and adherence to the rich cultural past of the country."[1] Girish Karnad in 'Author's Introduction' to his three plays also confesses to have inherited this tension which he believes is in the generation itself which he belongs to: "My generation was the first to come of age after India became independent of British rule. It therefore had to face a situation in which tensions implicit until then had come out in the open and demanded to be resolved without apologia or self-justification: tensions between the cultural past of the country and its colonial past, between the attractions of western mode of thought and our own tradition, and finally between the various visions of the future that opened up once the common cause of political freedom was achieved. This is the historical context that gave rise to my plays and those of my contemporaries."

This tension is present in each of his plays. Karnad's characters have aspirations in their minds and they strive hard to achieve them. But finally what they meet is contrary to their expectations. His major characters like Yayati, Tughlaq, Padmini and Basavanna strive hard to attain the desired end but cannot. As a result, Karnad's plots become the portrayal of dilemma, duality and tension.

Yayati presents a tension between Illusion and Reality. This is portrayed through a tale of struggle between two generations. In this struggle, on one hand is selfishness and on the other is sacrifice. Selfishness and sacrifice are two aspects of life which an individual cannot part with. When selfishness clashes with selfishness it leads to struggle: the play *Yayati* is the dramatization of this struggle. Yayati, the king, would always bear an illusion in his mind that he is a favourite king of his subjects and only he feels responsible for his people. He has a feeling that if he is given only a few years more he will complete the remaining projects of his kingdom. So the loss of his youth is basically the loss of his subjects. But the incident of borrowing youth from someone gives him a first jolt as no body from his subjects comes forward to sacrifice his or her youth for the sake of the king. His subjects, as Puru conveys to the king, hold that if the king has worked for their welfare they have paid the price for it in the form of taxes. Moreover, it was his duty as a king to serve them so he has done nothing extraordinary. Even his own son Puru is not willing to strike this deal. Rather, he smiles at his father's lot who wants to shift the responsibility of his actions on somebody else. Failing to find anybody else from the entire kingdom, Puru offers his own youth to his father. Puru too is under the illusion that his wife loves him so much that she will accept him even as an old man. But the reality shatters all illusions: Puru's wife (Chitralekha) becomes a reality figure to disillusion both Puru and his father.

When Sharmishtha informs Yayati for the first time that Shukracharya has cursed him with old age, Yayati's pride as a king collapses and he cries, "Old—Old! Old before night?" (46). Then he begins to show disgust not only for Shukracharya but also for Puru, his son, who he thinks can never be serious about saving him from the curse. He also abuses and curses Sharmishtha for behaving only as an "outsider" in his palace. She can't realize the magnitude of his sorrow, feels Yayati. Finding no way out, he falls on bed and "like a mad man" looks here and there. Searching for something, he spreads his hand. When Sharmishtha enquires what he is doing, he replies that he is catching hold of the past. Then he comments over the joys of his past comparing it with the present: "cursed moment. . . . I would enjoy the laughter and weeping would intoxicate me. So I would deliberately tease them and make them weep" (50). But now he feels helpless when Puru informs him that he can evade the curse if someone else comes to take it on his head, Yayati is beside himself with joy. He thinks, "Where is the shortage of the public for a Chakarvarti of Aryavati. There are soldiers, public and ministers. They all are obedient to me. However, they love me, I shielded them risking my own life" (53). But when it is reported to him that none is ready to make the sacrifice, he is unwilling to accept it and says, "what a madness to say so?" (53). But Sharmishtha justifies their refusal holding why they should accept the responsibility of someone else. This enlightens Yayati as even Sharmishtha for whom he is cursed does not side with him. He questions Sharmishtha, "What type of love is this?" as she is also not in favour of Yayati's shifting of responsibility to someone else. Again turning towards his son Yayati directs him to offer "full village . . . ten villages hundred villages . . . even half of his kingdom, anything they want" (55) for helping him. Puru informs him that he has already offered all these things even for a few years' lending of youth but none came forward. He rightly refutes Yayati saying that the question is not of sacrifice but of feeling responsible for one's actions. Like Sharmishtha, he too is of the opinion that he should leave for forest life. Now Yayati is a broken man:

> Puru, don't ridicule me. I hold your feet. Don't talk like this. It seems you don't have the realization of the magnitude of my sorrow. Don't laugh inhumanly. If the old age had come in its normal course of time, I would have had the courage to bear it. . . . This is a curse. . . . If I accept this curse, Puru just think, I would be left just with one

> choice . . . to go on and on. To return from such a path would be impossible. . . . But how to go on a dreamless path? (57)

Yayati is further disillusioned by his daughter-in-law, Chitralekha. She calls him a coward and asks him not to run away from being 'different' from what he expected others to be. Her argument shakes Yayati from top to toe: "(Smiling) When I accepted Puru I had no knowledge about him. I accepted him. You sucked from him the youth and the man who could continue Chandravansh from my womb. Now he himself needs support to work . . . the qualities I married Puru for are no more with him. But all those qualities are with you. You robbed your son of his youth. So this is logical to accept everything with it" (77).

Failing to cope with this unconventional attitude of Chitralekha, he terms it a "mean conduct." She urges him to break off the shackles of morality and culture. These customs and family rituals, feels Chitralekha, are the bindings of the society to control "the surging strength of the youth." The society uses these shackles lest the children grow up in a natural way "like trees and plants." So the cultural rituals are the "policies to control the new generation" (77). Chitralekha urges Yayati to take the initiative in this regard as she finds no reason in accepting these chains. But he does not have the courage to throw away these cultural bonds and becomes a dwarf before Chitralekha. He regards her revolutionary thoughts dirty which do not behove the daughter of Angkul and daughter-in-law of Bharatkul. But she refuses to bow to this conventional attitude.

Thus the play offers a tension between two generations: the old one is represented by Yayati and the new one by Chitralekha and Puru himself. If Yayati puts his rich cultural heritage above individuality, Chitralekha values individuality more than anything else. Puru too wants to be called by his own name only. He is an individual rather than the son of a king. When he enters the kingdom with his wife, Yayati asks him to feel proud because he has taken birth in a royal family. But Puru refuses it, "of course, I am born of a family of great men but I am simply an individual" (41). Yayati, at this, advises him not to be sarcastic about his family and be isolated from it, "Puru why do you have ironic tone when you are born in it. You should realize its greatness" (41). But Puru ridicules the idea of being fascinated by a few hackneyed tales about the bravery and swordsmanship of his father and forefathers. Failing to stand the mockery of his dynasty Yayati asks him, "What do you need? What do you want? Dynasty, education, respect, queen, what don't you have?" (42). Puru here makes it clear that he wants only to be Puru and not the son of a king. He tells his father how Chitralekha became his wife not because of being the descendent of Chandravansh. So he harbours a feeling that his wife is married to his father, not to him.

Yayati's ego as a king and a descendent of great dynasty gets punctured by Puru's individuality and his excessive faith in himself. Yayati fails to convince him why he should feel proud of those whom he has not seen and boast of those actions which he has not done. Yayati's words display the inherent tension between the two generations. "If we are together even for two days, it leads to controversy only" (43). To this Puru has an answer which forms the core of the problem: "I don't want to follow the path of my ancestors. I have a different way" (43). He does not want to be a god for his people but he definitely wishes to be something different which his ancestors could never be. He says that even his marriage was only to prove himself different from others. He is going to put the first child into the life of his father to "follow the ways of ancestors," but thereafter he will have his way. At this Yayati narrates the story of Swaranlata's husband, his Rath driver, who also wanted to 'have his own way' and be 'different' like Puru and ended up with suicide. But in Puru's view even attempting to be different from others is a great thing: "If one has the courage to question himself even that is enough" (44). He pities his father who can't understand his urges to be an individual. He feels that Yayati is "wearing a mask" behind which he doesn't want to hide his face. He does not want to be the object of his father's mercy either. He is sure that he does not lack anything to be an independent individual. It is his own identity which he does not want to submerge in his ancestral glory. His "hair stand on end" when his father offers him help for being weak:

> (Holding his hand) Stop father, stop. This mercy and this mask of pity does not behove you. The ill-will for me you have in your heart as a result of my conversation and conduct with you, should not be covered with mercy. It is against the tradition of Chandravansh. I have regards for your ill-will also but when you try to show pity my hair stand on end. (45)

He realizes that he as an individual is not at the mercy of anybody. It is only due to the feeling of personal identity that he is very curious to know about his origin. When Yayati sympathetically discloses that he is actually the son of a woman who had a Rakshasa-origin and has left deceiving everyone, Puru feels rather happy. He takes delight in his mother's rejecting his father's pride. But he curses his father for keeping it a secret from him for so long. He never repents over his Rakshasa-origin and proves his worth by taking over the curse of his father for which none was ready then.

This tension is carried over in *Tughlaq* who, like the king Yayati, is a disillusioned lot at the end. Muhammad realizes the vast gulf between his aspirations and his fulfillment, between the ideal and the real. There is a contrast between the ideal he has in his mind about his state and the reality he meets with the passage of time: "Tughlaq's suffering emanates from an unbridgeable gulf between aspiration and fulfillment, from the impossibility of communication, from an acute realization of the futility of human relationships."[2] Basically, the action of the play moves on two planes: one in the mind of Muhammad and the other outside him as in the Introduction to *Tughlaq*, U.R. Ananthamurthy writes:

> The external action throughout enacts the inner drama of Tughlaq. Both Tughlaq and his enemies initially appear to be idealistic; yet, in

> the pursuit of the ideal they perpetrate its opposite. The whole play is structured on these opposites: the ideal and the real; the divine aspiration and the deft intrigue.

The tension begins to appear from the beginning of the play. Two persons of opposite age, one young and the other old, are discussing the pros and cons of Tughlaq's regime. The old man has serious apprehensions about the emperor's style of functioning and is certain of the bad days ahead. The young man feels the other way round. His idea is that the country is in "perfectly safe hands—safer than any you have seen before" (147). Here the contrast is between the present and the past. If the young man is satisfied with the present, the old man feels to the contrary. The tension is also suggestive of India's present and her past. On one hand is the time of the British rule, and, on the other hand, is the time of independent India—the present. So the conversation between the old man and the young man reflects the tension between the past and the present of India. The old man does not approve of the present as he "never thought I would like to see a thing like this." But the young man thinks, "your [old man's] days are over" (147). However, the young man's illusion is hinted at when he is shown to be unaware of the reality which is known to the old man, i.e., Muhammad has usurped his father's throne and that was not an "accident" as the young man calls it. The young man in the second last scene is not so enthusiastic as is the young man in the opening one. Here the former simply questions and agrees to what the old man says. "Embarrassed" as he is at the end, he wants to be acquainted with the bitter reality which he never knew. He inquires from the old man: "Tell me more about this fort, grandfather" (193). Now he is not zealous and aggressive but is very receptive. He gives a very patient hearing to what the old man says.

The story of Muhammad's rule itself is the portrayal of tension. He starts with an ideal in his mind, "this country should have greater justice, equality, progress and peace—not just peace but a more purposeful life" (149). And his decision to shift the capital from Delhi to Daulatabad is an attempt to turn the ideal into the real. He hopes that after shifting his capital to Daulatabad he shall build an empire which will be the "envy of the world" (149). His idealism won't let him sleep peacefully. When his mother asks him about the reason why he cannot be at peace, his answer is that he is always dreaming about the bright future:

> I want to climb up, upto the top of the tallest tree in the world, and call out to my people: Come my people I am waiting for you, confide in me your worries. Let me share your joys. Let's laugh and cry together and then let's pray. . . . History is ours to play with—our now! Let's be the light and cover the earth with greenery. Let's be darkness and cover up the boundaries of nations. Come! I am waiting to embrace you all! (155)

From behind the idealism peeps the tension in Muhammad's thought when he admits the next moment that he cannot spread his branches in the stars as his roots have "yet to find their hold in the earth" (155). This lack of "hold" results in a reality which is dramatically opposed to his ideals. His dreams of peace and prosperity result in bloodshed and starvation. His slogans of honesty and fairness lead to treachery and falsehood. Muhammad frankly confesses the void between what he dreamt and what he got at the end: "And my kingdom is what I am—torn into pieces by visions whose validity I cannot deny" (165).

The reality spread before Muhammad is simply shocking for him. When persons like Shihabudin become victims of his sword, he is a frustrated lot. He fails to understand what he and his kingdom are heading for. The discovery of the conspiracy of his own murder jolts him. He laments, "What hopes I had built up when I came to the throne? I had wanted every act of kingdom to become a prayer, every prayer to become a further step in knowledge" (186). But every decision of Muhammad backfires. His own historian friend Barani begins to doubt the sanity of his decisions when he finds him murdering everyone who questions him. There is an atmosphere of total chaos all around, as Muhammad admits:

> In Ma'bar Ehsanshah has declared himself independent. Bahal-ud-din Gashtasp is collecting an army against me. The drought in Doab is spreading from town to town—burning up the country. Only one industry flourishes in my kingdom, only one—and that is the making of counterfeit copper coins. Every Hindu home has become a domestic mint; the traders are just waiting for me to close my eyes. (195)

He himself says that in the entire kingdom there are only two people he can trust, i.e., Ain-ul-Mulk and Shihab-ud-din's father. So he feels helpless in face of the turmoil all around: "What should I do Barani? What would you prescribe for this honeycomb of diseases? I have tried everything. But what cures one disease just worsens another" (196). Barani, smelling failures at all fronts, indirectly suggests to him to retire from the scene. But he won't do it in this life at least. He finds it rather hard because the "patient" in him cannot be cured and it cannot be left alone either. This is so because "there is no cure for his disease" (196). Muhammad, who was full of ideas once, feels helpless now:

> Don't you see the only way I can abdicate is by killing myself? I could have done something if the vultures were not so close. . . . I could have crawled forward on knees and elbows but what can you do when every moment you expect a beak to dig into you and tear a muscle out? What can you do? Barani, what vengeance is driving these shapes after me? (196)

Barani rightly asks him what has happened to his "ideas," and his stepmother laments, "How glorious you were . . . how idealistic, how full of hope. Look at your kingdom now" (204).

In the opening scene, Muhammad presents himself to be a secular and just king by honouring the judgement of Kazi-i-Mumalik. But the same Muhammad is shown to be honouring Aziz for murdering Ghiyas-ud-din Abbasid. This contrast reflects the total collapse of Muhammad's idealism. When Barani questions him for honouring a murderer, he replies that the idealistic words like justice have always eluded him and now he doesn't know if he is "pursuing a mirage or fleeing the shadow" (219). Finally, the idealistic king looks around dazed and frightened as though he fails to comprehend where he has reached. He is nowhere near the ideal that he had in his mind. Pramod K. Nayyar observes: "Girish Karnad's *Tughlaq* presents a tortured man. Muhammad Tughlaq is a king who wants to reform and improve his people. He is an idealist whose ideals' praxis renders him a dreamer and a fool. Tughlaq stands as a man deluded by his idealism and dreams."

The tension in *Hayavadan*a is between completeness and incompleteness. From human to semi-human characters, none is complete and everyone desires to be complete in one way or the other. Significantly, no one reaches the desired end and their pursuit to be complete leads them nowhere.

The tension begins to appear from the beginning with the invocation of Ganesha. The worship of Ganesha is done to wish success or completion of something. But Ganesha itself is not complete even to look at. It has a disfigured body: an elephant's head on a human body. Moreover, the god is shown to be riding a mouse and having a snake around its belly: snake and mouse are again at tension with each other. Thus, the atmosphere of tension is created in the very first scene. Soon we find, as introduced by Bhagavata, that the two youths who are our heroes lack completeness though they are 'perfect' in their respective bodies. Devadatta is comely in appearance, fair in colour, unrivalled in intelligence and has defeated the mightiest pandits of the kingdom in debates of logic and love, in poetry and wit. On the other hand is Kapila who is daring and matchless in strength and physical skills. Despite being so good in their respective fields they fail to get rid of the feeling of incompleteness. Not feeling content with the friendship of Kapila, Devadatta wants something more for his perfection and this vacuum is filled by Padmini, an exceptionally beautiful woman. Failing in love with her, he feels, "If only she would consent to be my Muse, I could outshine Kalidasa" (85), and that his poetry won't live without her. After he sees Padmini in the market he feels simply bowled over. Kapila acting as a mediator, Devadatta and Padmini become husband and wife. But the tragic side of the story is that Kapila too begins to feel incomplete without Padmini. Kapila's attachment to Padmini remains no more a secret for Devadatta. When he proposes to postpone the planned trip to the temple of Rudra, Kapila feels highly perturbed: "(Aside) So it's off. What am I to do for the rest of the day? What am I to do for the rest of the week? Why should it feel as though the whole world has been wiped out for the whole week? Why this emptiness" (94). This "emptiness" is caused by the supposed absence of Padmini, who, incidentally also feels incomplete even with the wit and poetic mind of Devadatta. This is because of her infatuation for Kapila that she won't let Devadatta cancel their trip though she is pregnant. When he proposes to cancel it on the ground of her pregnancy she outwits him: "What's wrong with me? I'm perfect. I had a headache this morning. But a layer of ginger paste took care of that. Why should we cancel our trip for a little thing like that" (94). Compared to her growing love for Kapila, the risk of her pregnancy appears to her 'a little thing'.

Of the three characters running in search of completeness, Devadatta and Kapila commit suicide. As chance would have it, Padmini happens to have the best combination: the head of Devadatta and body of Kapila. But she still feels incomplete. After Devadatta's body begins to change to the tune of his head, Padmini starts missing Kapila again. Compelled by his memories, she leaves Devadatta once again. She goes back to Kapila in the forest who is with the weakest combination, his own head and Devadatta's frail body. But they fail to find a permanent solution. This feeling of completeness becomes a mirage for them. She realizes at the end that their desire had taken them too far, where there is no way-out except death. Finding no escape, Devadatta and Kapila kill each other and Padmini prepares for Sati. The tension in the play is further heightened with the help of another character in the sub-plot, i.e., Hayavadana. It is neither an animal nor a human being. It has its own longing, i.e., to be a complete human being. But like the human characters, its desire also remains unfulfilled. With the grace of goddess, Kali instead of becoming a human being it becomes complete horse. Thus the story of incompleteness continues. The play which started with the idea of tension in the formation of Ganesha ends similarly. Commenting upon the tension in the play which appears to be universal in nature, M.K. Naik observes: "Padmini's plight suggests Woman's vain attempt to unite Man as intellect and as flesh in order to further her creative process. But these two aspects of the masculine personality are basically at war with each other and hence the attempt ends in destruction for both Woman and Man. Integration cannot be achieved by trying to reconcile the irreconcilable, but by accepting cheerfully the fundamental disharmony in human."

Tension in *Nagamandala* is between the patriarchal and the matriarchal view of woman's chastity. By presenting the two contrary views, the play mocks at the double standards adopted by the patriarchal society. Rani, a typical woman living in a male-dominated society, is married to Appanna, a wealthy village youth. He marries her and brings her to his house when she attains womanhood. She is married quite young like every Indian rural girl and continues to live with her parents until she reaches womanhood. Rani is a traditional woman married in a traditional way. Her attitude towards her husband after marriage is that of a traditional wife in a patriarchal society where husband is worshipped as a god. A wife cannot talk to her husband freely during day time. She is at the beck and call of her husband and has no authority to question him or his ways. He can treat her as he likes; he can go and enjoy himself with any man or woman.

Before marriage the girl in the patriarchal society grows up under the eyes of her brothers and father. Later, she comes under the vigil of a stranger whom she is married to. She has no choice in the selection of her husband. Thereafter, she is to serve him as a slave throughout her life. So woman in the patriarchal society is not treated as a human being but as a lifeless thing. In the name of chastity she sacrifices herself. As a critic observes: "Chastity is such a value invented by the patriarchal culture and accepted by women. It is one of the most powerful yet invisible cultural fetters that have enslaved woman for ages since the dawn of patriarchy. . . . The *Ramayana* in which Sita undergoes the fire ordeal to prove her chastity to Rama has been a cultural guide to Indians for more than two thousand years."[4]

The concept of chastity goes with and gets its indispensable strength from another morbid concept that sex is mean and sinful. Thus every woman in a patriarchal society is taught that chastity is more important than life: its loss and the resultant stigma are worse than death. It is because of this forced morality that the women undergo all sorts of oppressions. Those who raise a voice against it have to face the ire of society. Rani's fate is no better than that of a typical Indian woman who is always dominated by man.

A pertinent question which becomes the focus of attention in the play is the sexual liberty of the two sexes: male and female. Appanna, the husband of Rani, has complete sexual liberty whereas Rani is not allowed to talk to a person even of her own sex. Kurudeva describes her thus, "How beautiful you are. Ears like hibiscus. Skin like young mango leaves. Lips like rolls of silk." But Appanna has left her "wasting away at home" (32). Appanna has a concubine outside for whom he leaves behind his own newly wedded young woman waiting for him day and night. He visits her only once in twenty four hours only for his meals. Kappanna, the son of Kurudeva, has seen Appanna in his concubine's courtyard. Appanna's words in Act one, when we meet him for the first time, are marked by male chauvinism. He commands his newly wedded wife and treats her with the contempt of a typical male in a patriarchal society: "Have you brought in all the bundles. . . . Well then I'll be back tomorrow at noon, keep my lunch ready. I shall eat and go" (27). Rani reserves no right to question him as "He shuts the door, locks it from outside and goes away" (27). With Rani peeping out of the barred window he leaves her. She can neither talk to anybody nor can she go anywhere. She is only to cook for him like a servant. This is her plight as a wife in a patriarchal society. She even reluctantly accepts the 'root' which Kurudeva provides her to win her husband back. When she is preparing the mixture from the second bigger root she feels scared: "Oh my God! . . . How do I know this is not dangerous? Suppose something happens to my husband? What will my fate be? . . . Who knows . . . No, No. Forgive me, God. This is evil. I was about to commit a crime. Father, Mother, how could I, your daughter, agree to such a heinous act?" (37)

Thus she is conscious about her role as a devoted wife and a virtuous daughter. When Appanna faints after he is given the mixture of root, she starts crying. As a typical patriarchal woman, she cannot think against him knowing well that he is not sincere to her as a husband.

Karnad, in order to counter this male-chauvinistic vision, adopts a strange device in which the king Cobra develops sexual relationship with Rani. It is a fact that she develops sexual relationship with Naga taking it as her husband. Here rises an interesting question: Is Rani promiscuous? If she is, what about Appanna who spends nights with his concubine? Second, if Appanna has never been blamed for his extra-marital relationship, why Rani should be blamed when she develops physical relations with Naga only as her husband. Here Appanna's behaviour as a husband is a deliberate violation of social and matrimonial norms. So far as Rani is concerned, her act cannot be categorically termed as intentional. Still, she is to face the chastity ordeal. About her tragic plight, Smita Narula writes: "Rani is never free to express herself, to be herself. She is either daughter, wife, lover or mother. She is always playing a role imposed upon her, except in her dreams in the lonely nights that engulf her. She is a woman used, abused. She can neither live as a whore or a Devi. There is no element of 'person' for her."

The ordeal in which Rani has to prove her chastity is reminiscent of the fire-ordeal through which Sita proved her virtuousness as a devoted wife. If Sita was the victim of the male-dominance so is Rani. In the patriarchal society no such ordeal is reserved for a man however immoral he may be as a father, a husband and a brother. Rani too, like Sita, clears this hard test only to suggest a different concept of chastity. In reality, she cannot be said to have lost her chastity despite being impregnated by a man who was not her husband. Here, the concept of chastity is viewed from a broader aspect especially when the husband refuses to acknowledge his wife as a being with basic human desires.

If we divide the play into two parts: one before the snake-ordeal and the second after it, the tension between the patriarchal and the matriarchal views about woman comes to the fore. The first part is essentially dominated by Appanna who carries on his association with a concubine without bothering anyone and locking his own wife in a room. Rani in the first part is no more than an animal guarded by another animal at her door. She is only to wait for her husband and accept him as he is. He abuses and slaps her but she cannot dare to stand up against the oppression. She spends her marital life within the four walls of her house and still she is not liked by her husband. But after the snake-ordeal, exactly the opposite happens. Appanna confesses that he is a "sinner" and the Elders who had gathered to prove Rani a promiscuous woman fall at her feet. No body listens to Appanna now. He shouts desperately: "What am I to do? Is the whole world against me? Have I sinned so much that even nature should laugh at me? I know I haven't slept with my wife. Let the world say what it likes. Let the miracle declare her a goddess. But I know!" (60)

But these are the days of Rani now, Appanna has to forget all these things as Rani would do before the snake-ordeal. Rani too is in the know of the reality that the man before the snake ordeal was different: "no two men love alike . . . when her true husband climbed into bed with her, how could she fail to realize it was someone new?" (50) But despite all the apprehensions of the two about their past they start living together. Appanna starts worshipping her as a goddess, serves her like her attendant. His concubine becomes Rani's maid doing menial work in Rani's house. Now Rani can afford to love someone outside her marriage. She asks Appanna to give the dead Cobra a proper burial like the father of her son bothering least what Appanna feels as a husband. Appanna has no choice but to obey her: she has the full liberty which Appanna enjoyed in the first part of the play. But it is pertinent to notice that Rani is not as cruel and pitiless as Appanna was. Now, the question of chastity never arises between them. Perhaps they have started viewing the sexual purity merely a nuisance for them.

Karnad's *Tale-Danda* is another story of tension between the old and the new—on one side is the old rigid caste system and on the other side is the new concept of humanity in which all men and women are equal. On one hand is the old religion with superstitious practices like idol worship, and, on the other is the religion upholding human values. So the orthodox and the heterodox views of society come in clash with each other. One view goes by the origin of man holding that man is good or bad by his birth. The other view is that nothing is predetermined; it is the individual merit that determines his worth. So what matters is the individual not his social origin.

The old and the orthodox view of society is represented mainly by Amba, Bhagirathi, Sovideva, Damodar Bhatta and Bijjala—the king—whereas the new and the modern view is held by Basavanna—the saint and the other Sharanas like Jagadeva, Mallibomma, Sheelavanti, and Kalavati. The tussle between the old and the new appears in the beginning of the play. Amba, the traditional and orthodox woman, attends her ailing husband Shastri and is waiting for their son Jagadeva who has joined the Sharanas against their wishes. So Jagadeva here stands for sacrifice as he is fighting for the cause of the Sharanas at the cost of the love of his parents. Despite getting a message from his family that his father is in a serious condition, he prefers not to leave for his place as the honour of the Sharanas is at stake. He has to guard the treasury of the king in the absence of Basavanna against the conspiracy of the king's son, Sovideva. The Yuvraj was planning to open the door of the treasury in the absence of the treasurer, Basavanna, to defame him. So the Sharanas rally round the treasury. But for his presence, the Yuvraj would have manipulated the accounts of the treasury and ruined Basavanna's reputation as a saint. This incident would have spoiled the image of the Sharanas among the people.

When Jagadeva is about to enter his house with his Sharana—friend, Mallibomma, he is checked at the door by Bhagirathi, a Brahmin woman. She doesn't want that Mallibomma, who is a tanner by birth, should enter in a Brahmin's house. She doesn't hesitate to point it out: "This is a Brahmin household. Do you mind standing a little aside . . . what are we to do if you plant yourself on the doorstep like a feudal chieftain?" (3) But Jagadeva won't take it lying down. He answers back:

> This is my house, Bhagakka, and he is a friend of mine. My friends will come here when they like and stand where they choose. If that's not to your liking, you are free to stay as far from here as you wish . . . and mother you tell Mallibomma yourself. I won't set foot in the house unless he comes in with me. (3)

Amba has no choice but to permit Malliboma as she knows that her own son won't come into the house unless he does. She lets him enter though "she'll have the house purified later" (4).

Jagadeva takes it as his victory and announces to the onlookers: "Are you listening? All attention? This is my friend Malliboma. He is the son of a tanner and I am taking him inside our house. Are you satisfied?" (4) At this Malliboma feels "half-dead" because this is too big an incident for her to withstand.

Bijjala stands for complete selfishness and the Sharanas represented by Basavanna signify complete sacrifice and for them love for humanity comes first. Bijjala doesn't practise what he feels but the Sharanas practise what they preach. The king appreciates this humanitarian philosophy of Sharanas but he won't let them put it into practice. The Sharanas, on the other hand, preach that all men are equal and they implement this philosophy with the marriage of Shilavanta and Kalavati. About the ideology of the Sharanas, Bijjala opines that his wife and his son Sovideva cannot understand Basavanna. It is only Basavanna, realizes Bijjala, who acknowledges him as a human being which his forefathers tried to be but could not, despite their best efforts: "For ten generations they ravaged the land as barbers and for another five generations they ruled as the trusted feudatories of the emperor himself. Then they tried to change their caste by marrying into every royal family and even bribed generations of Brahmins with millions of cows to be Kshatriyas" (14).But they could not get rid of their low caste. As a result, Bijjala, despite being a king remains a barber for his people. So he is made to believe that "caste is like the skin on one's body. You can peel it from top to toe, but when the new skin forms, there you are again a barber—a shepherd—a scavenger" (14-15). On the other hand, caste has no meaning for the Sharanas, so "they sit together, eat together, argue about God together, indifferent to caste, birth or station" (15): there lies the difference between the two ideologies.

The contrast in Bijjala and Basavanna's vision of life also becomes the major point of tension. Unlike Basavanna, Bijjala has a narrow vision of life. He can't think beyond personal gains. He has brought the Sharanas in his territory not for any common goal but because they are hardworking people. For them, work is worship. Their belief in honesty and sincerity is to benefit Bijjala only. Moreover, he cannot think beyond blood relationships. For him only he and his family matters. He feels, "A son is the final goal of human existence . . . it may be that he drinks your blood and chews your bones to mash. But he is the one who'll keep your soul fed till eternity" (20). And he wants to inject this conviction into Basavanna's head. He preaches that man is not complete without being the father of a son. But Basavanna sweeps Basavanna's conviction aside with his saintly arguments. Bijjala feels that for man the blood relationships are important: "If men are set free from these blood bonds, they will merely sputter about like a pile of fish on the sand and die." But Basavanna thinks far beyond it. His realization is that it is not bare relationships that matter but the meaning one brings to them. In the final meeting when Basavanna asks him to believe in God's will, Bijjala expresses his inability. Basavanna advocates: "let's not try and bend God's generosity to our desires. Let His will be in that He has attended to you" (77). Implicitly, he asks Bijjala to trust in God but Bijjala finds it hard. The final meeting between the two ends upon a tone of victory for Basavanna, as Bijjala quotes him:

> He who runs is not a warrior
> He who begs is not a devotee,
> A warrior shouldn't run,
> A devotee shouldn't beg.
> I'll not run, I'll not beg
> O Lord of the meeting rivers
> Did I get it right? (77)

Basavanna nods in confirmation and then there is a "long pause."

The Sharanas' movement against the orthodox religion is itself marked by tension. Basavanna and Jagadeva represent two aspects of the Sharanas' movement. Basavanna stands for the Bhakti-aspect which is totally non-violent and spiritual while Jagadeva believes in 'tit-for-tat' policy. If Basavanna shuns violence in any form, Jagadeva defends Sharanas who occupied the Jain temple by force to turn it into a Shiva temple. It is only the Jains, Jagadeva feels, who had provoked the Sharanas to be violent. This sort of attitude upsets Basavanna. He dislikes violence for the sake of violence and also rejects superstitious beliefs among the Sharanas. Jagadeva believes and narrates to Basavanna that Ramayya, in Albur, did a miracle while attacking the Jain temple, as his head "flew in the air like pigeon." This unrealistic belief shocks Basavanna. He laments, "It is sad . . . even among the Sharanas, there is no shortage of credulity" (28).

Although Jagadeva believes in Basavanna's ideas of eradication of the caste system, yet he has not risen above individualism and fails to perceive Basavanna's philosophy in totality. He admits that he led the march to the treasury for his individual interest, i.e., to be "the talk of the town." He began to imagine himself being taken out in procession hoisted on the shoulders of his friends and companions. But, instead, Basavanna emerged as a hero as people say he performed a miracle" (30). This fans his feeling of jealousy towards Basavanna and he feels deceived. Moreover, when his father is thrown out from the service of the court by the king and he dies of this shock, Jagadeva "shrank, like a piece of soaked cloth" (30). He harbours personal feelings of revenge against the king. When Basavanna tries to pacify Jagadeva by saying that he should not arrive at hasty conclusion as he himself has left the king's service, Jagadeva misunderstands him and calls him a manipulator, actor and "conniving trickster." He quotes his father who advised him not to trust Basavanna as he is an "imposter." Thus Jagadeva's enmity with Bijjala has a personal touch while Basavanna is not against any individual but against the system itself. Jagadeva feels that he can bring change by killing the king; Basavanna knows that it won't solve any problem. The same happens when Jagadeva kills Bijjala against the wishes of Basavanna and that too by deception. Jagadeva and his fellow Sharana Mallibomma enter Bijjala's palace. In order to take him out from the god's room with a Linga in it, Jagadeva tells a lie that they have come from Kappadi. The king mistakes them as messengers from Basavanna. The moment he steps out of the room, he is struck by them. Even Jagadeva has no hesitation to follow him even into the sanctum but Mallibomma blocks his way. He wants to kill Bijjala only with an intention to emerge as a hero afterwards. He feels that if they don't kill him they will go down in history as "incompetent clowns." So with the fear of being a laughing stock in the eyes of the people, they attack Bijjala. All the companions of Jagadeva put their swords down and enter the sanctum. Taking Bijjala out and listening to his message for Basavanna, Jagadeva stabs him. Then he ironically addresses the dead body of Bijjala which reveals the tension between his and Basavanna's viewpoint:

> So this is your temple, Basavanna? These legs are pillars. This body the shrine. This head the gold copula. And yet how easily does the moving freeze into immobility. A stab—a blow and the river freezes. The blood clots, the body goes stiff. Look how this house of Lord Shiva shakes, rolls and pitches and all it needs is a sprinkle of blood. And a stab—. . . I am not afraid of sacrilege. Watch if you are Basavanna, Your Jaganna—The Solitary saint. (Then he stabs himself sitting in front of the Linga). (87)

The tension in *The Fire and the Rain* emerges from the very title of the play: Fire and Rain are two antagonistic elements. Here Rain is being desired through Fire and therein lies the tension in the plot. Girish Karnad says:

> Thus the phrase Agni-Mattu-Male in addition to counterpointing the physical elements normally seen as antagonistic, also sets up several other oppositions: between an Indo-Aryan (Sanskrit) and a Dravidian (Kannada) language between the pan-Indic and the regional points of view, between the classical 'marga' and the less exalted 'Desi' traditions, between the elevated and the mundane, and even perhaps between the sacred and the secular. (63)

So the major point of tension is between the 'elevated and the mundane' or the 'sacred and the secular.' The elevated and the secular are represented by the religious belief according to which the 'Yajna' is being performed. All those who are party to pleasing Indra, the god of Rain, by performing the fire sacrifice headed by Paravasu, as the Chief Priest, represent the sacred. The 'secular' is represented by the Actor-Manager, his limping brother, Arvasu, Nittilai and Vishakha. The two groups of characters move freely into each other's domain only to emphasize the tension between the two ideas. The opening negative sentence of the play by the king under whose supervision the 'Yajna' is being performed is in complete tension with the last sentence which is affirmative in nature. The opening sentence, "No, impossible! It's not possible" and the last, "It's raining: It's raining" are contradictory in terms. The man who was 'impossible' to enter the place of sacrifice makes the rain possible for which the king and his team were struggling hard.

The secular part that is presented in contrast to the fire-sacrifices is somewhat uncommon, i.e., the power of drama or of theatre. The playwright expounds the mythical significance of drama through the Actor-Manager. He says that Brahma extracted theatre from the four Vedas and combined it into the fifth Veda and thus gave birth to the art of drama. The god Brahma put further responsibility of theatre on Lord Indra, the god of skies. Because the gods cannot indulge in human practices, he assigned this responsibility to Bhart—a human being. Thus drama or theatre is also equipped with the background of gods and goddesses like any other religious practice.

After the fire-sacrifices fail to bear any fruit and the priests feel "dreary," the Actor-Manager with his limping brother and Arvasu stage a play along with the audience. Arvasu's acting is not given any metaphysical meaning; he is shown to be missing his beloved Nittilai even when acting. He is a man of earth with human feeling and desires. When Paravasu permits him to act as an actor, the first thing he misses is his beloved Nittilai. He wishes to have her sitting among his audience so that she could see him acting. His inner feeling is that the real theatrical activity is the mutual attraction between him and Nittilai. For Arvasu, their liking for each other is far better a theatrical activity than the mythical one. He tells Nittilai: "But you know, and brother knows, and I know that this isn't the real thing. This is a fiction borrowed from the myths. The real play began somewhere else. A month ago, a month? . . . You and I were going to get married. Begin a new life. And I had to meet the Elders of your tribe" (4). So real drama is the drama of life but not the one which is meant to please Indra. Thus, the real life gets the upper hand.

The conversation between Nittilai and Andhaka about the knowledge of Yayati rather intensifies the tension between the 'elevated' and the 'mundane.' Andhaka says that Yavakri has spent ten years to seek God and has the experience of seeing gods in person after mortifying himself and practising austerities. He narrates Yavakri's mystic experience thus: "ten years of rigorous penance and still Lord Indra would not oblige. Finally, he stood in the middle of a circle of fire and started offering his limbs to the fire—first his fingers, then his eyes, then his entrails and tongue and at last his heart—that's when the god appeared to him, restored his limbs, and granted him the boon" (9).

Nittilai very innocently but logically questions Andhaka whether Yavakri told him everything about his experience in the forest. Imparting his answer a spiritual touch, Andhaka says that a man of his status wouldn't talk about himself. Nittilai strikes at the weak point of this argument: "then how does everyone know what happened in a remote corner of the jungle—miles away from the nearest prying eye?" (9) And before Andhaka could make a rational answer to her question, she gives a second stroke, i.e., why are the Brahmins so secretive about everything? Comparing the Brahminical attitude with the ways of her own tribe that makes no secret of anything, she is critical of the former:

> You know, their fire sacrifices are conducted in covered enclosures. They mortify themselves in the dark of the jungle. Even their gods appear so secretively. Why? What are they afraid of? Look at my people. Everything is done in public view there. (10)

She further questions the validity of the knowledge given by the gods if they cannot help the starving: "My point is since Lord Indra appeared to Yavakri and Indra is their God of rains. Why didn't Yavakri ask for a couple of good showers?" (10) When men, women and children are dying of hunger, Nittilai finds it ridiculous not to make mention of it before the god of Rain.

Andhaka "half agrees" with her but defending his viewpoint desperately opines that such powers shouldn't be used to solve day-to-day problems. Finding a good opportunity to attack Andhaka's views, she gives a final blow to it. She questions the utility of such a knowledge which demands so much from a human being but is useless for human life. She poses two questions to Andhaka about Yavakri who is said to have gained the spiritual knowledge. Her first question is if Yavakri can save the dying children by making it rain for them. Second, can he tell when he is going to die? So if he can neither save the dying children nor does he know the moment of his own death, then there is no use of gaining such a hard-earned knowledge.

The tension in the play gets further strengthened with the characters who possess opposed natures. Nittilai is a humane and compassionate character in contrast with the like of Yavakri and Paravasu. Yavakri is a revengeful and cruel man bent upon using his knowledge against nature and humanity. Nittilai has a sympathetic heart and proves it by helping Arvasu when he is badly beaten up and is thrown out from the sacrifice premises by the king's soldiers. The soldiers kick him, drag him and tear his shroud thread calling him demon. It is only Nittilai who nurses his wounds and helps him with fruit etc. She cares for him like a true beloved. We see her mopping up his vomit, wiping his bottom "like a baby" (45). Moreover, she never compels him to marry her.

When she asks him to live together she doesn't mean that they should live like lovers or like husband and wife. She is ready to live with him even like his sister. Arvasu too pledges not to ever marry any other girl. Nittilai even soothes him and asks him to forget the humiliation he has met at the hands of his brother.

In contrast to the selfless and virtuous world of Nittilai, Parvasu, like Yavakri, emerges as the embodiment of vice. First he violates the religious norms of the sacrifice by slipping away to meet his wife, then he kills his father. He even wrongly punishes his own brother calling him "demon" for being murderer of his father. Arvasu rightly puts it, "Yavakri, and father and brother [Parvasu] can bring out the terrors from the womb of the earth and play with them. They can set the foul nature against you" (43). Furthermore, about Parvasu's heading the sacrifice, he feels, "But if such an evil man continues as the chief Priest of the sacrifice, it'll rain blood at the end" (43). Nittilai, on the other hand, will never approve of the contamination of evil only because someone else started it. She suggests to Arvasu to leave the result of the sacrifice "to the gods." She asks him silently by her logical and humane mind. She says that Yavakri avenged his father's disgrace by attacking his sister-in-law, then his father avenged her by killing Yavakri, and Parvasu killed his father and if he too wants revenge there is no end to it. She asks him to kick the world aside which calls him "unregenerate sinner" and stay clean as he is. Arvasu still bears a grudge that his humiliation was conspired by Parvasu, Yavakri and even his own father because he wanted to marry her throwing all traditions to the wind. The other two are dead and he will not spare Parvasu, says he. Nittilai calls it "nonsense."She not only helps her lover by guiding him at this juncture but also helps the starving people who are dying because of no rain. Even the Actor-Manager feels indebted to her for helping his hungry children. She helps everyone whether they want food, nursing or even her laughter. In this way, Nittilai proves herself to be the contrast of all those in the play who nurse a feeling of hatred and jealousy for others. She, with her humane nature, becomes the exact opposite of Yavakri. He makes a prophecy about the death of Nittilai saying that she will die within one month; Nittilai also makes a prophecy but it is about life not about anyone's death: "I am sure your dancing will bring the rains. Goodbye" (52). About the tension in the characterization, Pramod Mutalik holds: "Parvasu and Yavakri are out to please Indra to attain their personal goals through austere paths. Yavakri's tall claim of knowledge of the soul of the universe (Brahmajnana) and the hypocrisy of Parvasu are exposed and ridiculed by simple life-loving human beings—Nittilai and Arvasu. These qualities render them far superior to Yavakri and Parvasu."[5]

Nittilai creates another tension: the tension between mortality and immortality. She does not like Indra, the god of rains, as he is immortal and those who do not have fear of death cannot enjoy life. Life loses its meaning without the fear of death, feels Nittilai. She rightly puts it thus, "When someone doesn't die, can't die what he can know about anything? He can't change himself. He can't—can't create anything" (51). She likes Varitra because he, despite being triumphant according to the story in the myth, chooses death. She further elaborates her point, "I always wonder—if the flowers didn't know they were to fade and die, would they have ever blossomed?" (52) When Arvasu wants Nittilai back in his life as he feels she died for his sake, Indra warns him of consequences in disturbing the order of nature. If the wheel of time rolls back, says Indra, Yavakri, Raibhya, Parvasu and all those who died on earth would also come to life along with Nittilai. This will result in unprecedented suffering. Before Arvasu's wish is granted, Brahman Rakshasa also appears for his release. He tells them his own story of suffering which is the result of his immortality. At this Arvasu, remembering the compassionate nature of Nittilai, asks for the Rakshasa's release. He knows that Nittilai herself would have made the same choice: she would prefer the release of Brahman-Rakshasa to asking for

Rain or for her life. Here god Indra fails but Arvasu who also represents Nittilai after her death wins as it rains at the end. Thus the play ends again with a tension: who is more capable to do good for human beings? Can immortal gods do everything and mortal human beings are insignificant?

NOTES

1. R.K. Dhawan, "Girish Karnad, the Man and the Writer," *The Plays of Girish Karnad: Critical Perspective*, p. 13.
2. Veena Noble Das, "Search for Tradition in Kannada Drama: The Plays of Girish Karnad," *Modern Indian Drama in English Translation* (Hyderabad: Taurus, 1988), p. 143.
3. M.K. Naik, "From the Horse's Mouth," *Dimensions of Indian English Literature* (New Delhi: Sterling, 1984), p. 196.
4. M. Sarat Babu, "The Concept of Chastity in Nagamandala," *The Plays of Girish Karnad: Critical Perspectives*. p. 237.
5. Pramod Mutalik, "Fine Tribute to a Master Playwright," *The Deccan Herald,* 6 June, 1999.

Techniques

Girish Karnad's experiment with 'tradition' is not limited only to the treatment of themes. In his techniques too, he makes bold experience with devices of classical and folk drama. Like other modern playwrights Girish Karnad is not content with the existing dramatic forms. The urgency of doing something new impels him to find a new form. In order to constitute the desired form, he explores the traditional theatre devices of his own land and that of Europe. As a critic says, Karnad "employs in his plays the techniques of classical and folk theatre in India. He makes use of the devices of the culture to expose its retrogressive values." The judicious synthesis of classical, folk and contemporary devices results in a new dramatic technique. Because of his experiment with the conventions like the use of chorus, music, mime, songs, curtains, unrelated comic incidents, mixing of human and non-human world, use of masks and narrator-actor device, he is sometimes close to the typical Karnataka-theatre and sometimes to Brecht for breaking the illusion of theatre and appealing to the reason than to the emotions of the audience. In Karnad's words:

> to me three kinds of theatre between which I swiveled and moved and written, the company Natak on one side, the Yakshagana with mask-like appearance, its ritual atmosphere, and thirdly the kind of theatre which really is a naturalistic theatre, the western theatre as one came to see it, hate it, dislike it, but was impossible not to be possessed by it.[1]

Role of Sutradhar and Bhagavata

Sutradhar in *Yayati* and Bhagavata in *Hayavadana* are devices derived from the classical Indian drama. There Sutradhar, as the chorus in Greek drama, plays the role of an introducer or a commentator. Known by different names in the different regional varieties, he holds the most important position in the Indian folk theatre. In a way, he may be called the focal point of the evaluation of folk theatre itself. In the Yakshagana theatre of Karnataka, he is respectfully called 'Prathma-Vesha'—the first character. More or less, he performs the same function as those of the ever-present Greek chorus.[2]

The play *Yayati* starts with the appearance of Sutradhar who, as the stage lightens up, starts introducing the plot saying, "I am Sutradhar." Going to the story of the plot and its characters, he informs the audience about the Puranic origin of the play. In a philosophical way he relates the plot of the play with the real life of the audience, saying:

> Sometimes when we are walking around a path we see two paths in front of us. We can follow one and feel that we are fulfilling our life's purpose. However, we are always conscious of the inaudible voice which says, what would have happened if we had followed the other road. . . . Yet let the untrodden road be untrodden and let its secret remain buried. Let us stick to the morals of the grandmother's stories that we heard in our childhood. This is the sad story of our life. (8)

Arousing the interest of the audience, he reminds them of their duty as well: "All the different characters after putting down the bags of their sins and noble actions have come to take rest. To have a look at them in our job, this is our play" (10). Acting as a mediator between the authors and the audience thus, he bows out and the play starts. After this, Sutradhar does not appear on the stage again.

This role of Sutradhar is played by Bhagavata in *Hayavadan*a but with more variety. Basically, there is a difference between the role of Sutradhar in the classical Sanskrit drama and that of Bhagavata in the folk theatre. Bhagavata, the modified version of Yakshagana, remains present on the stage throughout and is responsible for the development of action. Karnad deliberately follows this folk device. The choice of Bhagavata, the narrator-actor, from the folk drama leaves the playwright with more choice to diversify with the action of the play. In order to transcend the limitations of time and place, the playwright also uses the folk devices like the Female-Chorus and the inanimate Dolls.

Apart from being the introducer like Sutradhar in the beginning, Bhagavata is also a commentator and an important character in the play. He intervenes in the action as per the wishes of the playwright. Along with the Female-Chorus and the Dolls, he is a source of irony, comedy and seriousness in the play. He appears as a commentator and analyzer of action at very crucial moments. Imparting a sense of shock to the audience, he makes them intellectually participate in the action.

Like a classical play, *Hayavadana* starts with the worship of Ganesha. This convention of worshipping Ganapati, in the beginning of every auspicious work, comes straight from the scriptures. Since, according to the 'Natyashastra,' drama itself is a religious ceremony—a Yajna—the worship of Ganesha has travelled to the theatre also. With this conventional use, Karnad makes use of Bhagavata, another conventional device. Interestingly, the fusion of the two old devices begins to serve contemporary purpose. The sacred importance of the invocation gets lost when Bhagavata questions Ganesha's formation. He says that "the Ganesha has elephant's head on a human body, a broken tusk and a cracked belly" (75). Thus a question is raised in the very beginning about the modern man, i.e., the feeling of his incompleteness.

The play starts in the manner of a folk tale as Bhagavata says, "this is the city of Dharamapura, ruled by the king Dharamsheela whose fame and empire have already reached the end of the eight directions. Two youths who dwell in this city are our heroes" (73). Then parity between the main characters Devadatta and Kapila is established with the statement, "The world wonders at their friendship." As he is interrupted by Hayavadana who starts telling his own story as an omniscient and intelligent communicator, Bhagavata brings the audience back to the earlier point by singing, "Two friends they were. . . . They saw a girl and forgot themselves. But they could not understand the song she sang" (82). Thus, he also hints at the constraints of the two friends and the fate of Padmini, the female character.

The family background of the characters that Padmini is the daughter of a leading merchant of Dharampura and Devadatta is a man of learning is shown to the audience by Bhagavata only. After informing the audience about the marriage of Devadatta and Padmini, he appears only when Act II starts. About the dispute 'who is the actual husband of Padmini?' he poses a direct question to the audience, "what indeed is the solution to the problem?" (40) Breaking the theatrical illusion he asks the audience to have a ten-minute break for tea. Then we find Devadatta relaxing and sipping tea on the stage itself. After the dispute is settled by the Rishi, again he announces, "So the roads diverged, Kapila went to the forest and disappeared and never saw Dharampura again whereas Devadatta and Padmini returned to Dharampura and plunged into the joys of life" (111). To give a finishing touch to the play and raising symbolic, ironic and comic value of it, he prays to lord Ganesha, for a grandson to a grandmother, a smile to a child, a neigh to a horse. Joined by the other characters, he prays:

> Grant us, O Lord, good rains, good crop, prosperity in poetry, science, industry and other affairs. Give the rulers of our country success in all endeavours and along with it, a little bit of sense. (139)

The reference to the 'rulers of our country' gains significance when it is related to the opening scene of the play which shows that the stage is "empty except for a chair . . . and a table" and only a mask is seen on the chair.

The female-chorus is made to speak for Padmini. Being an Indian wife she cannot say, "A head for each breast: A side for each arm" (82). It defends the reality of woman's carnal desires and justifies Padmini's liking for Kapila. When her body is set ablaze at the end, the Female musicians sing a chorus replete with ludicrous beauty, "our sister is leaving in a palanquin of sandalwood . . ." (40). With this device at the end, the scene remains no more emotional but the institution of marriage stands mocked at. The Sati-scene loses its tragic effect.

Use of Dolls

Another modern experiment done with the folk-theatre device in *Hayavadana* is the use of the Dolls. Apart from revealing the inner psyche of the characters, it also provides off-stage information. The Dolls inform the audience about metamorphosis in Devadatta's body, "His palms! They were so rough, when he first brought us here. Like a labourer but now they are soft. Soft like a young girl's" (116). Then they inform about the reveries of Padmini for a man who is not her husband: he is not "very nice, rough like a labourer. But he has got a nice body—looks, soft" (118). Further, the audience find the Dolls arguing, fighting bursting with giggles on the stage. When Devadatta picks them up to throw them away as they are torn, Doll I sarcastically comments, "cover your wife before you start worrying about our rags" (121). Thus, they become serious, comic and ironic as the situation demands.

The Story

Sutradhar in *Yayati* and Bhagavata in *Hayavadana* become one in *Nagamandala* and appear as the Story. The role of the Dolls is played by the Man and the Flames. It is only the Flames that inform the audience that the story is made of one known to an old woman since long but she never narrated it further. Feeling choked, it planned to come out from the open mouth of the sleeping woman. The Story takes the form of a young woman and the Song becomes her 'saree.' The young woman wrapping herself in the saree stepped out and moved to the temple where other flames had assembled. In the play, the story performs a very crucial role, e.g., when Rani prepares a mixture from the roots to give it to her husband, the Story guides her to put it on the anthill. This suggestion becomes a turning point in the plot. On the other hand, the Flames have their own role to play. They twice sing a song—when Rani has sexual encounter with Naga and when she waits for him after he stops visiting her being wounded by the mongoose. The employment of the device of using Flames and the Story as characters have great dramatic significance, as Girish Karnad himself says in an interview:

> What is interesting about the lamps telling the story is the fact that I intend to explore and depict the meaning of creativity. Story-telling is creativity. . . . In fact the whole play is about the story which wants to be told. It is not my story, I did not create it. It was already there—as the deconstructionists say—and the play simply creates devices for the telling of that story. Drama is not for me a means of self-expression. Drama can be production of meaning also. The story has an autonomous existence. The function of the artist is to create a world for the story to happen and then, if possible, to interpret it.[3]

The use of the Flames or the Dolls in *Hayavadana* also reminds us of the traditional puppet theatre in India. The puppet theatre is of such a great antiquity that India is called the home of the puppet play. Ancient Indian literature, including the great epics, frequently refers to puppet plays: "Not only string puppets and shadow puppets but also the mechanical puppets capable of presenting dramatic shows are mentioned in the ancient theatre. . . . India has a long and rich tradition of puppet theatre."[4] Like Bhagavata's folk style the Story starts, "A young girl . . . she was the only daughter." Then she comments intermittently for the convenience of the audience. Commenting on the passage of time she says, "And so the days rolled by" (28). Thus, she is important in herself guiding the characters and the audience at times. The cobra becomes her lover only when, guided by her, Rani pours the mixture on the anthill. Then it addresses the audience direct like Bhagavata, saying, "As you know, a cobra can assume any form it likes, it entered the house through the bathroom drain and took the shape of Appanna" (38). After this begins the double role of Appanna. The Story also informs about the death of her dog, mongoose and the absence of Naga for fifteen days. In her commentary, the Story leaves room for doubt about Rani's perception of Naga's identity: "she applied her ointment to the wounds, tended them. But she never questioned him about them. . . . Needless to say, when her husband came during the day, there was no scar on his face" (49). Then, after Rani is declared a goddess, the Story tends to finish up the play. The discussion that goes between the Story and the Man about the ending leads to the resumption of story. The Man says that the night is not over yet, hence, the danger of death still hangs. The conversation between the Man, the Story and the Flames shows the central role they are to play in the development of the action:

> Man: (exasperated) These Flames are worse than my audience. Can't they wait till the story is over?
> Flame1: But is not it?
> Man: It can't be. No one will accept this ending.
> Story: But why not?
> Man: Too many loose ends. Take Kappanna's disappearance for instance.
> Story: Oh, that's Kurudavva's story. I am only Rani's story. (59-60)

S.R. Jalote observes that Man is the metaphor of the playwright and his critical faculty, the story is that of his poetic imagination, and the Flames stand for both the village women and the audience.

Use of Prologue and Epilogue

Girish Karnad's use of Prologues and Epilogues puts him very close to the modern playwrights like Bernard Shaw. In their own way, both the techniques contribute towards the development of thought. In *Nagamandala*, the Prologue introduces a man who is sitting lonely in a temple and is yawning "involuntarily." Turning to his audience, the first sentence he says on the stage is, "I may be dead within the next few hours." Then, after a long pause he utters, "Actually dead. I might die right in front of your eyes" (22). With long pause in his opening speech on the stage, he creates the atmosphere of melancholy and alienation. This melancholic tone is intensified with the arrival of Flames which after being put out in the villages gather in a temple. The stories they narrate of their respective household together with that of the Man become the precursor of the alienation that is to follow. After Flames are introduced in the Prologue their further appearance on the stage does not astonish the audience. They provide them very vital information. For instance, when Naga and Rani are lying together in tight embrace, they surround them and sing a song of joy. Finally, it is only after they question the sad end of the play that the Man resumes the story when the actual narrator has gone. It is only because of the curiosity of the Flames that the Man gives a finishing touch to the play. Thus, he assumes the status of a playwright who creates a story of his own.

The Prologue used in *The Fire and the Rain* also provides the background to the main action of the play. The device of irony and the use of supernatural elements are introduced in the Prologue itself. It presents some of the main characters like Paravasu, Arvasu, Nittilai, the king, the Actor-Manager and his brother in the beginning. The important issue of the play—the fire sacrifice versus theatre—comes to the fore in the Prologue itself. Putting the Prologue and the Epilogue together there emerges an independent plot which attains added meaning only after being resisted to the rest of the play.

Invocation and Use of Mask

Since Karnad's style fuses classical and folk convention within the framework of contemporary theatre strategies, the invocation of the deity and the use of mask come together in *Hayavadana*. It starts with the bringing of the mask of Lord Ganesha on the stage. Though the invoking of Ganesha is like a typical 'Yakshagana' play (an open air performance taking themes from scriptures with Bhagvata as its chief actor), yet the idea of the mask of Ganesha raises a logical question as well: it is a fact that head represents body then how can a god with animal's head be better than human beings?

The mask is also used for Hayavadana, the main character in the sub-plot. Bhagavata, blaming him for wearing a mask of a horse and scaring people with his absurd appearance, asks him to put it off. As he does not budge, Bhagavata pulls at Hayavadana's head with both his hands. When he fails, Natta—the actor—also comes to his help. Now the actor holds Hayavadana by his waist while Bhagavata pulls at the head. This tug of war continues and Hayavadana cries as the pain becomes unbearable. Finally, the truth dawns on Bhagavata, i.e., "this is not mask! It is his real head" (78). This Yakshagana device is further used to project the essential opposition between Devadatta and Kapila. Devadatta wears pale-coloured mask but that of Kapila is dark in colour. The mixing up of their heads at the temple of Kali becomes possible only through their use. The goddess is also wearing the mask which shows her terrible in appearance. This idea of mask contributes to the basic theme of the play, i.e., every man wears a mask which results in the complexity of human relationship and the feeling of alienation. As regards the other folk devices like the use of curtains, half curtains, painted curtains, stage-hand and miming, *Hayavadana* sets another precedent. In view of the fusion of tradition and modernity in this play, Veena Noble Dass remarks, "*Hayavadana* is an innovative experiment that offers a new direction to modern Indian theatre. This experiment proves that the traditional forms need not be treated as precious artifacts, but can be adopted to treat modern themes suitable for the urban Indian audience. Indeed theatre is changing and the old and the new form mingle and renew themselves. This new cross fertilization between the realistic westernized urban theatre and folk theatre seems here to stay."

Use of Light and Sound

Along with the use of mask, Karnad's *The Fire and the Rain* presents a perfect fusion of music and light. In the Prologue after Paravasu permits the theatre troupe to perform a play, we see Arvasu carrying a mask. The Actor-Manager and his limping brother are accompanied by a couple of women who are to provide music. The moment the Actor-Manager starts singing benedictory verses the stage "darkens" and only Arvasu is left in a "pool of light" (4). In Act I, after the scene between Arvasu, Nittilai and Andhaka is over, the stage darkens again for a contrasting effect. Now the light comes up in another part of the stage representing the hermitage of Raibhya. Vishakha is seen filling water in a metal urn. The long scene between Vishakha and Yavakri, when he stops her standing in the middle of her path and wins her over, is also enacted in the light. On the other hand, when the Brahmin-Rakshasa summoned by Raibhya runs in the direction of Yavakri, the lights fade out. It is completely dark on the stage when the Brahman-Rakshasa kills Yavakri and Andhaka cries over his dead body. As the Epilogue starts and Arvasu wears the mask, there is a roar of drums in the background. Similarly, light and music are sometimes collectively used. When Indra appears on the stage it is preceded by the "melodious music" and "soft and gentle" light (53).

The modern devices as of the sound-light effect remain an essential device in the other plays as well. Karnad's first play Yayati starts with the slow lighting up of the stage. As darkness begins to fade out, the slow music is heard in the background which gradually becomes louder. "The music goes on for two minutes" (7) before Sutradhar appears. As he raises his hands to introduce himself and the action of the plot to the audience, "the music begins to subside away and finally comes to an end" (7). Similarly at the end of his speech before he leaves, "The stage darkens up slowly. Again it is lighted up gradually" (10) as we see

Devyani sitting on a bed with Swaranlata by her bed-post. Thus use of light and sound enhance the dramatic effect of the play.

The use of light, miming, freezing and quick shift of scenes, remain distinctive in *Nagamandala.* As the play starts it is night and "Moonlight seeps in through cracks in the roof and in the walls" (22). On the moonlit stage we see the Man and the Flames talking. In Act one, the stage is lighted up to show that it is the day time. But, as Appanna leaves Rani and she is left alone talking to herself, "Her words become distinct as the lights dim" (27). Again it is dark on the stage. The scene shifts into night and Rani is found dreaming of her parents. As she gets up, "it gets light" (28). She mimes splashing water on her eyes. Appanna also comes and he mimes taking a bath in the bathroom: taking of bath is always staged through miming.

The moment Appanna goes out Rani falls asleep and the stage gets dark. Kappanna and Kurudavva also appear in the dark. As Act II starts it is again night and Naga is seen caressing Rani when she is asleep. Whenever Naga appears it is always dark as against Appanna who appears on the lighted stage (showing day time). Rani's disclosure to Naga about her pregnancy is followed by the sudden splash of light. They both freeze and the "lights change sharply from night to mid-day" (52). Now Naga turns into Appanna and starts beating Rani. When he goes to the village-Elders the lights change into night again. Rani is found crying as Naga sits by her on the floor. Again the stage is lighted up and the scene changes into the village square.

Music and light play an important role when Rani is declared a goddess. As the cobra slides up Rani's shoulders and spreads its hood on her head and moves over her shoulders looking like a garland, "music fills the skies. The light changes into a soft, luminous glow" (58). The Elders shout, 'Palanquin! Music!' Later, Rani gently takes Appanna in her arms. Again there is music in the background and they speak to each other in inaudible voice. When Naga, summoning his magical powers, enters Rani's tresses, "a beam of light is thrown on him" and "the rest is plunged into darkness" (62). As he ties a tress into a noose and places it around his neck, the stage slowly becomes dark. Music is again played in the background when Appanna kills the cobra and Rani, filling her eyes with tears, presses it to her cheeks. At the end it is not dark on the stage as it was at the beginning of the play. It is morning now, the "sunlight pours in through the cracks" (65). Thus use of light and sound helps the playwright in the sudden shift of scenes too. The cobra, dog and mongoose involve puppetry which reaches its climax of excellence in a scene in which the snake kills the dog at Rani's door. Thus the device of light and sound is frequently used by the playwright to achieve specific dramatic purpose.

Use of Spectacle and Other Dramatic Devices

The use of spectacle remains a special feature of Karnad's plays—spectacle refers to all visual aspects of produced scenery, lighting, costumes, make-up and movement of the action. If a father's youth and son's old age act as a major spectacle in *Yayati*, Appanna in double role in *Nagamandal*a and mutual killing by Devadatta and Kapila and then their coming back to life again in *Hayavadana*, the death scene of Bijjala in *Tale-Danda* and the play-within-play in *The Fire and the Rain* are spectacle creating elements indeed. Karnad's *Tughlaq* is also full of spectacles. The personal appearance of Muhammad in striking costumes, announcement of the shifting of capital, call for banning prayer and revival of it, the march of the Amirs towards Delhi and especially the sudden shift of scenes give a spectacular effect.

Other devices like 'silence' and 'pauses' are also a special feature of Karnad's dialogues. Pauses in a dialogue serve more than words and mark a silent interplay of conscious and unconscious motivation. In *Tughlaq* the meeting between Muhammad and Sheikh-Imam-ud-din is punctuated by pauses. The long silence during their dialogue speaks of the crooked motives of the emperor. Similarly, his studied pauses are noteworthy when Muhammad is to inform his mother about the death of the Sheikh. In *Nagamandala* too the opening speech of the Man is full of pauses which reveal his sad state of mind, his fear of death and his frustration as a playwright. They set up a mood for Rani's sad story. In *The Fire and the Rain* when the Actor-Manager and the courtier are convincing Paravasu to let them play a drama along with the fire sacrifice, the dialogues are again marked by pauses. The first meeting between Vishakha and Paravasu when he visits his wife after seven years is also noteworthy in this regard:

> Vishakha: How are you, husband?
>
> (*No reply*)
>
> Only occasional bits of news about you. When someone here goes to the city and attends the sacrifice.
>
> (*No reply*)
>
> Are you well? Or do you still drive yourself to the point of illness-like a demon?
>
> (*No reply*)
>
> I was sure you wouldn't come home even if I were on my death-bed.
>
> (*No reply*)
>
> But my fornication was reason enough, wasn't it?
>
> (*No reply*)
>
> Whatever you heard about Yavakri and me was no rumour.
>
> (*No reply*) (31)

This one-sided dialogue tells a lot about the speaker as well as the listener. The former is curious to express everything in one breath without making any pretence as she meets her husband after a long time. On the other hand, the latter is caught in the dilemma of being the chief priest and the husband of Vishakha. He feels helpless and fails to respond positively to her expressions. Vishakha's dialogues are punctuated with pauses especially when she narrates her story of woes, that is, how she became the object of her father-in-law's wrath.

Use of Irony

As a modern playwright, irony and comedy are Karnad's favourite devices. He makes use of situational, verbal and dramatic irony. To start with the first play of Karnad the major events upon which the whole action is based grows on ironic grounds. Yayati, the king, readily develops physical relationships with his attendant (Sharmishtha), but is adamant not to accept Chitralekha's hand. At the risk of his life he shares a bed with Sharmishtha but refuses to accept Chitralekha as his queen which involves no physical risk at all. Moreover, he feels all-concerned so far as his subjects go but when his own daughter-in-law exhorts for his youth to be taken care of; he retreats and pays no care to her exhortations.

The encounter between Yayati and Sharmishtha is ironic: Sharmishtha starts as Yayati's attendant and ends up as his queen. At the beginning of the play she begs of Yayati for help to end her suffering. As her suffering came to an end, Yayati accepts her as a queen, he loses his youth: the end of an attendant's suffering results in that of her master. Sharmishtha's career from Devyani's friend to her attendant and from Devyani's attendant to her rival in love is full of irony. On the other hand, Yayati's fall from being the saviour of Devyani to the seducer of Sharmishtha along with his longing to remain young, is deeply ironic.

The relationship between Yayati and Sharmishtha provides an ironic analogy to that between Puru and his wife. Yayati is Sharmishtha's master and she is his attendant but they have sex on the same bed meant for the newly wedded Puru and Chitralekha. It is rather ironic that the father (Yayati) becomes younger than his son (Puru). Furthermore, the newly wedded Chitralekha failing to continue with her marital joy commits suicide, but an attendant is able to win over the king and accompanies him to the forest. Anantpur, which is being decorated in the opening scene for the reception of the newly wedded couple, faces death of the same bride. The daughter-in-law teaches a lesson to her father-in-law and that too through her death.

Irony in *Tughlaq* begins to appear from the very beginning. Tughlaq's proclamation is, "My beloved people, you . . . have seen for yourself how justice works in my kingdom—without any consideration of religion or creed" (153). The situation turns ironic when we learn that the winner against the king is not actually Vishnu Parsad but Aziz disguised as Vishnu. This ironic situation results in comedy when Aziz, mimicking a public announcer, says, "Henceforth the people may file a suit against the Sultan for the misbehaviour of his officers. . . . Justice will be done" (152). His comments are a source of laughter when he justifies his disguise before Aazam: Had he not been disguised as a Brahmin "Then what would happen to king's impartial justice. A Muslim plaintiff against a Muslim king—where is the question of justice? Where is the equality between Hindus and Muslims?" (153). Thus, the disguise of Aziz ironically puts the whole administrative system under Muhammad Tughlaq upside down. Muhammad's slogans of justice and equality sound hollow and appear comic to the audience.

Karnad's *Tughlaq* presents the best example of irony through comparison and contrast. If we compare the views of Muhammad with those of Aziz there emerges an interesting contrast. If Tughlaq is an idealist, a dreamer and is deaf to the public views, Aziz is a realist and every inch a practical man. If the court's judgement in favour of the disguised Aziz makes a mockery of Muhammad's slogan of secularism and justice, the underground life of Aziz and Aazam mounts a parody on Muhammad's ideals about the welfare state. Aazam's and Aziz's re-appearance in the camp on the Delhi-Daulatabad route and their routine presents a contrast between what Tughlaq claims his kingdom to be and what it actually is.

To Muhammad's manipulative power, wit, foresightedness, secretiveness and ruthlessness, Aziz provides an ironic parallel.

Like him, from the very beginning Aziz is clear about what he is to do. First of all he manipulates the king's decision to compensate those whose land has been confiscated by the state. If Muhammad feels everything will be settled after he reaches Daulatabad, Aziz's destination is also the same but his purpose is different. He tells Aazam, "There is money here and we will make a pile by the time we reach Daulatabad" (155). If Muhammad has disguised himself as a religious and kind emperor, Aziz, basically a washerman, is disguised as Brahmin. He appears like a Brahmin and ends up as the special messenger. The incident, when a Hindu woman with a dying son in her lap requests Aziz for medical help and he remains unmoved, reminds of the cruelty and corruption of Muhammad. Aziz expects money from her knowing full well that her husband is bedridden. When Aazam asks him why he does not let her go to the doctor, he stoically says, "It is a waste of money. I am doing her a favour" (188).

For Muhammad and Aziz, politics holds a common interest. Aziz's remarks about politics are ironically true:

> Politics! It is a beautiful world—wealth, success, position, power—yet it is full of brainless people, people not with any ideas in their head. When I think of all the tricks in our village to pinch a few torn clothes from people—if one uses half that intelligence here, one can get robes of powers. It is a fantastic world. (190)

Like Muhammad he also makes use of religion and caste for his selfish ends. He knows that even if the Hindu woman is not allowed to leave the camp, she cannot complain against him. Complaining against a Brahmin to a Muslim, according to the Brahminical dogma, will send her to hell. His encounter with Ghiyas-ud-din also proves him a cruel man. Like Muhammad, he murders him without a touch of humanity. His singing and dancing after killing Ghiyas-ud-din reminds of Muhammad's neurosis. Putting on his robes Aziz asks the horrified Aazam, "How do I look, eh? The great grandson of the Khalif. . . . Laugh, you fool laugh. Celebrate! What are you crying for? . . . Dance,

dance . . . (sings)" (201). He aptly defines himself before Muhammad, "I insist. I am your majesty's true disciple" (216). Indeed, Aziz appears as his 'shadow' or the other Muhammad. It is perhaps because of this parallelism between them that Muhammad pardons him even for his grave crimes.

Similarly, Aazam represents the coward and the foolish in Muhammad. Despite taking adventurous and bold decisions Muhammad appears as a sacred man. We see him bowing before his subordinates requesting them to pray for his success. Aazam too resembles Muhammad in his frank confessions. He admits that he is a common pickpocket and is not of sharp intellect. He, like Muhammad, emerges as a helpless person. Being a coward at heart many times he disapproves of Aziz's behaviour. But he does not leave him easily either. Finally, when Aziz kills Ghiyas-ud-din, he literally cries and laments: "God! God! Why did I stop him? Why did not I let him go?" (201) and I'll die of freight here" (212). Aazam's bribing the two servants of the palace to bring two horses so that he and Aziz could run away, angers Aziz over his foolishness.

The prayer scene in which the attempt is made to murder Muhammad also provides the irony of situation. It is Muhammad who has made prayer mandatory for every Muslim. But the same prayer proves a danger to his life. Moreover, it becomes reminiscent of Muhammad's action of killing his own father during prayer. Similarly, the encounter between Muhammad and Aziz, when the latter is disguised as Ghiyas-ud-din, illustrates the irony of situation and comedy through contrast. With his presence of mind and witty dialogues, Aziz appears to eclipse Muhammad's intelligence. When it occurs to Aziz that he can deceive Muhammad no more, he at once reveals his identity. The moment Muhammad asks him who he is, Aziz retorts, "I am a dhobi from Shiknar. My first name was Aziz. There have been many others since then" (215). At Muhammad's warning that he should not overreach himself, Aziz responds, "I don't. But since your majesty came to throne, I have been your most devout servant. I have studied every order, followed every instruction, considered every measure of your majesty with great attention" (216). Keeping in view his past, Aziz's remarks are highly ironic. Muhammad's every ideal including his plan to introduce new currency stands mocked at in front of his eyes. Aziz says, "Soon after your Majesty introduced the new copper currency. I succumbed to its temptation. . . . There is enough money in that business, but too much competition, soon it become unprofitable" (217). Finally, when Muhammad abuses him calling him a 'dhobi,' he very cleverly replies, "What if I am a 'dhobi,' Your Majesty? When it comes to washing our filth no saint is a match for a 'dhobi'" (218). The washerman fascinates the king so much that he is forced to confess, "This man is a genius" (218) Ironically, none appeals to the emperor throughout his kingdom but a criminal washerman. U.R. Ananthamurthy puts it thus:

> He [Muhammad] is aware of the irony of his life when Aziz, the only character in the play who has skillfully used all the schemes of Tughlaq for his own designs, kills Ghiyas-ud-din and comes in his guise as a holy messenger of peace to purify land and revive the banned prayer. The irony is deeply tragic. In the end Tughlaq and his kingdom are one in their chaos, and he knows it.

The basic irony in *Hayavadana* is that all the major characters are leading a double-life until it is too late to merge their own two selves: they dare not confess openly what they feel at heart. Like Tughlaq they are more concerned with their appearance, i.e., what the others feel rather than what they actually desire. No wonder, they want to remove the gap between the appearance and reality on one pretext or the other, but they cannot. Padmini loves Kapila but does not want to let Devadatta know; Kapila loves Padmini but he does not want it to be known by Devadatta. Devadatta dislikes Kapila's presence in his family after marrying Padmini, but he won't tell Kapila. The bold initiative to break the dual structure of their relationship is taken by Padmini when she goes to the forest to see Kapila. But it is too late now. So the gap between their true selves, what they pretend and what they actually experience, results in irony. We see 'Lava and Kusha' or 'Krishna and Balrama' or 'Rama and Lakshmana' killing each other and the Sita (Padmini) witnessing the duel and then performing 'Sati'.

The scene at the temple of Kali provides an irony of the situation along with humour. After the heads are joined on wrong bodies, the involved characters have full laughter. Even the words of the goddess Kali cause subtle humour:

> The rascals! They were lying to their last breath. That fellow Devadatta—he had once promised his head to Rudra and arms to me! . . . Think this Kapila, died right in front of me—but 'for his friend.' Mind you! Didn't even have the courtesy to refer to me. (103)

At this crucial moment, the goddess feels "sleepy" and is "yawning." Without being much concerned she leisurely asks Padmini what she wants. When Padmini prays for saving her as she has lost her husband and his friend, Kali's comment is ironic, "I know I have done that already" (102). She expresses her inability to listen to her for too long as she is "collapsing with sleep!"

By comparing the mood of the two, Kali and Padmini, the playwright is sarcastic about the human plight in front of the gods. Padmini has a grudge against Kali that if she knew before hand what their fate had in store for them, then why she did not intercept in time to save them. To this Kali's reply is both comic and ironic, "if it hadn't been that she was sleepy, she would have rather thrown them out" (103). Like Devadatta and Kapila she herself is burning with jealousy. Even Kapila died, she feels, not for her sake but for the fear of being accused of his friend's death. Despite knowing well about their intentions and their future she remains a mute witness to their suicides. The goddess asks Padmini not to drag her into it as she had nothing to do with them. Moreover, even after Padmini joins wrong heads the goddess does not respond to her cries. When, at the end, Kapila and Devadatta kill each other in a duel and she is left all alone, Padmini's remarks are sarcastic, "Kali, mother of all nature you must have your joke even now. . . . As the other women die praying that they would get the same husband in the next life, she has not been left with even that hope" (131). Here the playwright is ironic about the roles of the gods and goddesses in human life.

Hayavadana, the main character in the sub-plot, also serves the ironic and comic purpose. Apart from being an object of attraction and laughter with his human body and animal head, Hayavadana is another instrument of irony in the hands of playwright. In his pursuit for completeness he has run from pillar to post. He has tried every god at Banaras, Rameshwar, Gokran, Haridwar, Gaya, Kedarnath and "even the Dargah of Khwaja Yusaf Baba, the Grotto of Virgin Mary" (81) But none could help him.

Finally, as suggested by Bhagavata, he goes to try Kali of Mount Chitrakoot. As happens in Padmini's case, it rather aggravates Hayavadana's problem. Instead of becoming a complete man he becomes a complete horse and that too with the human voice. Having tried all the gods, he finds hope in loudly singing the National Anthem because, "I have noticed that the people singing the National Anthem always seem to have ruined their voices—so I try. But--but—it—it does not seem to work" (137). Through Hayavadana, Karnad satirizes the Indian leaders who sing the National Anthem loudly more for show than out of any patriotic feeling. The playwright's stroke of irony is at its best when no god but Padmini's child helps him to be complete. He gets rid of his horse-voice by laughing with the innocent child. The ironic picture becomes complete when Hayavadana who wanted to be a complete man ends up as a complete horse. To quote Bhagavata, "unfathomable indeed is the mercy of the elephant-headed Ganesha. He fulfilled the desire of all. . . . How indeed can one describe the glory in our poor disabled words?" (136)

In *Nagamandala*, as the play starts, the Man—a playwright—who is supposed to keep the audience awake is himself trying hard "to pry open his eye lids" to avoid sleep. Sitting in a "ruined temple" and swearing by "the absent God" he presents an ironic picture of life. Like the goddess Kali in *Hayavadana,* Naga, the god of fertility in Hindu mythology in *Nagamandala*, plays an ironic role. If Kali complicates Padmini's problems, Naga, the god of fertility, deceives Rani by disguising its original identity. The play starts on a note of dramatic irony when the audience knows that the man who spends nights with Rani is not actually her husband. Ironically, the god of fertility seduces an innocent newly wedded girl by acting as her husband at night. It not only impregnates her but also helps her in passing successfully the purity test. With the superhuman Naga the adulterous Rani emerges as "the goddess."

The snake-ordeal which Rani undergoes to prove her marital purity provides irony of situation. Naga, the seducer of Rani for whom she has been labelled "adulterous" by her husband, acts as her guide. Caught in a moral juncture Naga commands Rani, "Now, do as you are told—When I come and go at night, don't go out of this room, don't look out of the window, whatever the reason and don't ask why?" (45). He knows that if he behaves politely Rani may complicate the problem for Naga and for herself. Like any sincere lover, he feels a moral responsibility to take Rani out of this great crisis. With his 'kind' help, the adulterous Rani becomes the "Divine being." With an illegitimate child in her womb Rani becomes a goddess and Appanna has to cut a sorry figure in the court.

This ironic tale does not end here. The king cobra feels angry and jealous like the goddess Kali: when the cobra sees Appanna and Rani sleeping together it burns with jealousy, "No I won't bear this. Someone must die, someone has to die" (61). Feeling jealous over Appanna's privilege as a human being, he curses himself: "Her thighs, her bosom, her lips are for one who is forever a man. I shed my own skin every season. How could I even hope to retain the human form?" (61) Then his entering into Rani's tresses to be an integral part of her body is his last superhuman effort to be a part of a human being.

The wishfulfillment of Rani, as of Padmini, is the handiwork of the irony of fate. Padmini mixes up the head unintentionally and goes with the much desired body of Kapila, similarly Rani pours the root-mixture on the anthill and gets the much desired nights through the king cobra. It is the goddess Kali in *Hayavadana* and the blind Kurudavaa in *Nagamandala* who become instrumental in changing the fates of the heroines. The basic irony in the play is that man (Appanna) behaves like an animal, and the animal (Cobra) behaves like a man. Moreover, the blind (Kurudavaa) acts as a guide and Rani, meaning queen, is treated as a slave.

Irony in *Tale-Danda* also springs from comparison and contrast. Jagadeva and Sovideva, both belonging to the new generation, provide ironic contrast to each other. Both have to fight and struggle but their goals are different. Jagadeva fights for a social cause and for this he leaves his home. He revolts against his orthodox parents who believe in the caste system. Sovideva, on the other hand, fights for his personal gain. He desires to be the "natural heir" of Bijjala. So both the characters are poles apart as regards their attitude to life.

If Jagadeva fails to attend to his ailing father it is because of his commitment to the Sharanas' cause. As regards his respect for his parents that cannot be questioned. Sovideva, on the other hand, is a very arrogant son. His only aim in life is to be in power by hook or by crook. He desperately motivates his mother against Bijjala: "You are a princess of the Hoysala dynasty, Bijjala's favourite queen. And I am your only son and what do I have? A jangling bell to keep me occupied" (8-9).

Similar is the contrast between Basavanna and Damodra, the priest. Both represent religious views of life, one is broad in vision, the other is narrow. If Basavanna is a saint-philosopher who believes in human and spiritual values without believing in idol worship, Damodra is a priest who defends caste system in the name of religion. When Basavanna talks of the equality of human beings he is called "treacherous" and "obstinate" by Damodra who supports Sovideva wholeheartedly to crush Basavanna and his ideology. Provoking Sovideva against Basavanna, he says, "If one wants to catch a tusker, one must dig a pit enough to take him in entire" (9). He is more worried than the king about the inter-caste marriage advocated by the Sharanas. He takes it as a danger to him as a priest and to his Brahmin-class. So he calls this inter-caste marriage an "unnatural alliance." He appears more as a social-miscreant than a religious preacher. He poisons Sovideva's ears against the Sharanas by spreading rumours:

> The whole city is like tinder-ready to ignite into flames. The citizens have vowed to stop this unnatural alliance at any cost. A hundred mercenaries arrived from Sonnalige this morning. . . . A band of fighters from Tulunadu is getting in Kannamma's rest house . . . our information is that the Sharanas too are spoiling for a fight. Houses have turned into armories. It is impossible to predict which way the wind will blow (55).

Thus Damodra surcharges the social atmosphere as a villain. He advocates that the inter-caste marriage is a "desecration" of the body of "the Primordial Man," the source of the four varnas. When Indrani counters him saying that the Sharanas have done so much for the downtrodden and the destitute, Damodra's reaction is ironical, "Our caste is like one's home meant for one's comforts, one's traditions" (56). He fails to answer when questioned about those who suffer because of this inequality.

When Sovideva accompanied by the priest surrounds the king in his own palace, Damodra's words speak of the actual villain in him. The language he uses for Bankamma to suggest that the latter is the king's sycophant proves that the caste-feeling has killed the man in him. He looks more a buffoon than a priest: "Bankamma accompanies the king on his way to the fields in the morning.

Carries the pot of water to wash his Majesty's behind. The king has constipation and his bowls tighten, he responds benignly to every suggestion. So this whipper snapper has virtually ruled the king" (60).

When Kallapa is killed he justifies his killing saying that the reason of his death is that he could not be corrupted. Siding with Sovideva he urges the king to crown his son with his own hands, but denies to mean any treason against the king. The king has no doubt about the villainous role the priest is playing. He says, "This game is yours I concede that" (64). Thus, his character is in complete contrast to that of Basavanna who is transparent and truthful in his actions.

Bijjala is imprisoned by his own son and he is waiting for the Sharanas to come up. It is a fine illustration of the irony of situation. Earlier, he would always threaten Sharanas of eradication from his kingdom and would always criticize them. But now he is expecting them to turn up for his help. Reaching the palace Basavanna asks him to 'Trust in God' but Bijjala still declines. Despite treason by his own son and sincerity shown by Basavanna, he fails to embrace Basavanna's view of life. His faith in his kingship remains intact. He consoles his wife saying that he will be the king again and she the queen. Still he learns no lesson and fails to recognize what is wrong and what is right. Then the scene at the sanctum in the palace is even more ironical. Bijjala who has been a non-believer in religion embraces the Shiva Linga to save his life from Jagadeva and his men. They try hard to wrench him free but fail. Bijjala gives a loud laugh and calls it a miracle that he is doing so for the first time. His comments are ironic, "Basavanna could not make me bend before the Lord. My wife could not, but you young whelps have made me cling to it" (86).

As in the other plays, *The Fire and the Rain* has irony inherent in it: the fire is used in the play as an instrument to bring rain, the true lovers (Arvasu and Nittilai) are beaten up and one is killed, the men with universal knowledge use their power against the fellow human beings, finally Indra is pleased with the performance of an ex-communicated man (Arvasu). It is only Arvasu whom the Lord of rain tells to ask for a boon. Ironically, Paravasu's resolve to please Indra parallels Arvasu's effort to please Nittilai. The moment Arvasu is permitted to stage a play he invokes no heavenly body but his love. The playwright puts Arvasu and his love at a higher pedestal when Arvasu says that the "real play" started when he and Nittilai were going to get married. Paravasu, whose responsibility as the chief priest is to see that there is no error either of omission or commission, himself leaves the fire sacrifice at night to meet his wife. He falls prey to the feeling of jealousy and revenge against his father. After killing his father he joins back as the chief priest. He commits one more sin by accusing his younger brother of patricide and beating him up for the sin he has never committed. The chief priest (Paravasu) ends up more as the chief sinner in the play. In an interview with Ratnottama Sengupta Girish Karnad remarks about the irony in the plot: "What interested me was these norms of Hindu Religion like tapas, doing penance or the fire sacrifice to please the gods. And the people, who do these penances, continuously break the moral norms. A sage who does tapas rapes a woman. Another doing a sacrifice in a temple kills his father."

The second irony is that if the king and Paravasu are conducting the fire sacrifice to please Indra, Indra himself is conducting the same ritual to kill his brother Vishwarupa. The same religious ritual is being used for different purposes by human beings and the gods. This contrast between the human and the superhuman enhances irony in the play. Like Paravasu disliking Arvasu's entry in the Yajna-premises, Indra dislikes that of Vritra. This parallelism between the gods and the human beings gives an ironic twist to the play that results in comedy:

Varitra: Indra is treacherous.
Vishwarupa: But, Vritra, you know that I have extracted from him a

promise not to hurt me.

Upa: They say gods should never be trusted.

(*Laughter from the audience*)

Vritra: Indeed it is said that when the gods speak to us, the meaning they attach to each word is quite different from the meaning we humans attach to it. Thus, their side of their speech often denies what our side of their speech promises. (*applause*)

Even their silences have double meanings. Hence the saying that the thirty three gods occupying the heavens make for sixty six silences. (*Laught*er) (55)

Finally, it is ironic that Indra appears before Arvasu who has never wished to see any god. In the dialogue that takes place between Indra and Arvasu, the gods stand fully exposed. They are not omnipotent as human beings think them to be. The Brahmin Rakshasa similarly shows Arvasu higher than the gods, "You can understand the pain and suffering and the gods cannot" (61). Rightly so, Arvasu asks Indra for the release of Rakshasa but "nothing happens" (62).

In the victory of Arvasu lies another irony, i.e., he who pleases Lord Indra is basically a loser at the hands of society. He has lost his Brahminhood and his beloved too. In the presence of everyone Arvasu is knocked down by Nittilai's brother and Nittilai's throat is slashed by her husband. She lies in the sacrificial pavilion dying like a sacrificial animal. Here Arvasu's comments reflect the cruel and inhuman attitude of society towards its individuals: "Serves you right! Who asked you to meddle with this world? . . . No one'll weep for you. Nittilai. Not even me. I'll sing no lullaby of hate for you" (58). Lifting her corpse on his shoulder Arvasu goes into the burning pavilion, then the voice of Indra is heard: Indra appears when Arvasu has lost everything. About Indra's appearance, he has a very logical question: "Indra? But what do I have to do with Indra? I seek only death" (59). Nothing can be more ironic than the situation that Arvasu never wishes to see Indra but he does; he strongly wishes to have his Nittilai back in life but he can not; he wants the release of the spirit but it does not take place; he has never desired rain but it comes.

Apart from using the irony of situation and the occasional use of its dramatic form, verbal irony is frequently used in all the plays by Girish Karnad. In *Yayati* after the king has seduced Sharmishtha and Devyani smells out this new relationship between the two, she ironically remarks, "Very Good! You inaugurated Anantpur well. This sort of inauguration could have not been made even with the blessing of a god" (31). Similarly, at the close of the play when Chitralekha dies after taking poison, Sharmishtha taunts Yayati by calling her death the "first victory" of his second youth. Puru says, "It appears as if you [Chitralekha] were called here only to die" (52). In *Hayavadana*, when Bhagavata learns that Kapila is living in the jungle, he refuses to accept it. Equating men with animals, Kapila ironically remarks, "Beasts do why not men?" (122). In *Nagamandala* when Naga asks Rani to speak something and not to sit silent, she says, "You talk so nicely at night. But during the day I only have to open my mouth and you hiss like a stupid snake" (42). She never knows that it is actually the snake who she is talking to. The verbal irony becomes the source of comedy in *Tughlaq* when Aziz asks Aazam if he has heard the royal performance the other day. Aziz answers back, "which one? There are so many?" (152). About Shihab-ud-din's compliment to Muhammad that he is just and impartial, Rattan Singh says, "Yes indeed, who can deny that! He is impartial! . . . Of course Hindus as well as Muslims are dying with absolute impartiality" (172).

Sometimes the sarcastic comments of the characters about the policies of Muhammad become comic too. About the heavy taxes levied on the people a character says, "Look at what is happening in Delhi. Just look at it. You cannot take sleep without tax for it. You cannot even cheat without having to pay" (174). In *Tale-Danda* too, similar ironic strokes are employed. When the priest says that nothing utilized in the post-funeral ritual of Jagadeva's father should be used, the latter questions, "But I too was used in the rituals. So what to do with myself" (33). At this, the priest is left without any answer. Similarly, *The Fire and the Rain* is also full of ironic expressions. The last dialogue between Vishakha and her husband at night says a lot about the play. She asks him to kill her, "for all your experiments you haven't yet tried the ultimate," to which Paravasu responds, "You are right. I must. You are still my guru" (33).

'Story-within-the-Story' Device

The 'story-within-the-story' device like that of the traditional theatre is a typical feature of Girish Karnad's plays. They are sometimes meant to divert attention from the main plot. Studied closely, they become an integral part of the play. In *Yayati* Swaranlata's story that she narrates just to "fill up the gap" is of the sort. She tells Chitralekha that she was the only daughter of her father. She would serve food to a poor Brahmin who, in return, would teach her. He would come to her place, teach her at night and would leave in the morning. Then she got married and spent ten years in perfect marital bless. One day her husband learnt about the poor Brahmin's association with her family. Despite repeated assurances by her, his doubt grew and he started losing his sleep at night. By going to other women he tried to take revenge on her. Still, peace of mind eluded him. Agony and self-torture became a way of life for him. Failing to witness his suffering, Swaranlata told him a lie, that is, the idea of losing her virginity to the Brahmin was a fact. With this false confession her husband got rid of the agony caused by suspicion. This story of Swaranlata is of every character in Yayati. By narrating the story of her past, she falls in line with the other characters. Her tale resembles that of Sharmishtha, Devyani and Yayati. Every character suffers because of one or the other reason. Sharmishtha suffers because of Devyani, Devyani because of Yayati, Chitralekha because of Puru and Yayati because of his own actions.

The story of Hayavadana also fits well into the basic pattern of the play. Hayavadana says that his mother was the princess of Karnataka. When she came of age her father invited the princess of all the kingdoms so that she could herself choose her bridegroom. The prince of Araby riding a white Stalin came too late. On seeing him, Hayavadana's mother fainted and when she woke up she said she wanted to marry the white horse the prince was riding. Married to the horse, she stayed with it for fifteen years. One day in place of the horse there was a celestial being, a "gandharva." This celestial being was cursed to be born as a horse by the god Kuber because of his misbehaviour. After fifteen years he again turned into his original self. He asked his wife to accompany him but she refused. He cursed her for this and she became a horse. After turning into a horse she went away leaving Hayavadana alone. Reeta Sondhi also finds similarity between this tale of the princess with that of Padmini: "Her sub-conscious is as agile as her 'conscious.' As for her total personality, her earthliness is alluring, her desire of perfection is compelling and her waywardness in wanting to shape her own destiny is as overwhelming as the parallel tale of the princess who chooses a horse for a mate. This tale emphasizes the wild eroticism of Karnad's heroine. Even Hayavadana—son of the princess referred to—suggests her aspiration for the intellect. At the end of it, when she fails in her second desperate attempt at attaining the unattainable, she still triumphs. Defeat in itself has no meaning. Here, somewhere, somehow, Karnad has come back to his Indian sensibility."[5]

Moreover, the idea of marriage by choice, the role of the supernatural, the idea of blessings or curses, the departure of husband and wife and the abandonment of child are important common features. The idea of incompleteness and complexity of relationships is the basis of the story. Interestingly, after becoming a horse, Hayavadana's mother runs away "happily." Her joy is on account of the meaninglessness of human life. Apart from this psychological significance, it has also the socio-religious relevance. Like a common Indian, Hayavadana visits different religious places to pray for his completion. But no god or goddess can help him. Towards the end, the description of Hayavadana running around the stage and searching for completeness replicates a stereotyped life.

Nagamandala also has a similar story narrated by Kurudavva. It is about Kurudavva's getting three pieces of root from a mendicant and getting married with their help. Apart from keeping the right balance between pathos and comedy, the story of Kurudavva also furthers the main action. As Kurudavva says that she was born blind, so none was ready to marry her. Her father went from village to village to find a match for her, but all in vain. One day, when she was alone, a mendicant came to their place. To his heart's content she served him with hot food. Pleased with her service he gave her three pieces of root and said "anyone who eats one of these will marry you." When someone distantly related to her family came to stay with them, she gave one of these pieces to him which led to their marriage. Then she gave birth to a son named Kappanna. Here Kurudavva's desire for marriage coalesces with Rani's desire to win her husband for her marital bliss. Incidentally, the piece of the same root solves Rani's problem too. Moreover, Rani is also blind like Kurudavva, metaphorically though not physically, to the activities of the cobra from whom she has a son too. Kappanna also needs a female partner. Towards the end we see Kurudavva weeping as she has been left alone by her only son for some girl who used to beckon him every night. Explaining the relationship between the story of Rani and that of Kurudavva, Karnad says:

> What happens in the main plot is Rani's—a woman's—search for a man who is her lover and not her husband. But it is not a problem of adultery since the lover is a serpent. This situation adds a non-human dimension to the problem. In the sub-plot the son leaves his mother and the girl, like the serpent lover, comes from some other world.

> She is a Yakshini. The blindness of the mother in the sub-plot is genuine, but the blindness of Rani is ambiguous. She is deliberately blind to her infidelity. This is how I have tried to juxtapose these two plots in order to create a complex of meaning.[6]

What seems to mark all the sub-plot by Karnad is the desire of every male and female to have union with the opposite sex. This common feature merges up the main and the sub-plot almost in every play.

The Fire and the Rain also brings forth the example of 'play-within-the-play.' By staging 'The triumph of Lord Indra' the playwright once again adopts the mode of traditional theatre. Basically, the play dramatizes the scene of Brahma's attempt to murder his brother Vritra. But the story of the relationship between Brahma and Vritra and the fire-sacrifice arranged by the former to kill the latter has many things in common with the main action of the play. Indra, like the other main characters in the play, appears to be suffering from alienation. He is burning with jealousy against none other than his own brother. He nourishes a feeling against him: "Everyone admires Vishawarupa, everyone sings his praise . . . which makes me feel like the eclipsed moon" (53). To kill his brother and clear his way to supremacy, he organizes a 'Yajna' in honour of his father Brahma. The king arranges the fire sacrifice to save his people from the famine but the god Indra arranges it to kill someone. We see that the chief priest and Indra both commit patricide. Apart from this, Brahma's murderous attack on his brother reminds of Paravasu assaulting Arvasu when he tries to join the fire sacrifice. This similarity between 'play-within-the-play' and the main action serves the ironic and thematic purpose.

Comedy and Humour

From its inception, humour is inextricably associated with theatre. "Even the early theatre in the form of primitive tribal rituals and magico-religious ceremonies had elements of humour.

Recreation and magic were also aspects linked with humour to the early manifestation of ritualistic drama."[7]In this regard, Girish Karnad's plays are also no exception. In *Tughlaq* the conversation between Aziz and a man who acts as the guard for the dead bodies in Muhammad's palace has a woman and six kids with him. When Aziz asks him what he is going to do till the Sultan arrives in Daulatabad, the man's innocent and comic reply is that first of all they will get married because they could not get time for marriage in Delhi. Similarly, when Aazam says he is fed up with his life Aziz suggests to him to commit suicide. Aazam's answer is, "Tried once, went and jumped into a well. But the cold water cheered me up so much that I had a good swim and went back home" (197). At the next moment, he laments why he is a thief and cannot live in peace like others. The comedy turns into the tragedy of a common man who also wishes to live peacefully.

In *Tale-Danda* too there is a comic incident in scene II when Bijjala and Sovideva are found kicking Kallapa only to prove their worth as a ruler. First Bijjala orders his son Sovideva to kick Kallapa on his back. Despite several attempts he fails even once to kick him. To prove his worth as a king, Bijjala in anger starts kicking Kallapa that sends him reeling and crashing to the floor. This is no doubt a comic scene but Bijjala's remarks make it satirical as well: "Now, in order to be a ruler, what is the primary qualification? Surely the ability to kick people around. That's why they say to be born a king in this life you need to have been a donkey in your last" (12). Similarly, in scene II when Bijjala is waiting for Sharanas and they don't turn up, he feels worried and restless. Going into the sanctum to see them in the sky light, he orders his attendant Mariappa to step into the god's room. He helps the attendant climb up to the wall but he keeps slipping by. As there is no ladder the king asks Mariappa to climb over his back. Now this becomes highly comic but satirical too: the servant standing on his master's shoulders. Feeling threatened by his own son Bijjala says, "That's not high enough. Stand up. Go on. I won't drop you (laughs). I am your sovereign after all. I bear the burden of earth on my shoulders. I won't drop you, I promise" (Mariappa stands on Bijjala's shoulders with the support of the wall) (74-75).

Symbolism

Karnad makes free use of traditional and personal symbols to build up his thought. His concern for the inner problems of man and his revolutionary outlook towards old values disposes him to employ different symbols at different places.

The recurrent reference to 'Chess' in *Yayati* and *Tughlaq* makes it a symbol of the complexity of human relationships and the feeling of alienation. In *Yayati*, Sharmishtha calls mutual relationship between Yayati, Devyani and herself very 'complex.' She feels that death is the only way out for her. Yayati too feels roped in this game, "Now I come to know that I am also a Mohra [pawn] in this game" (25). After being a friend to Devyani and then serving her as an attendant, Sharmishtha feels "tired of playing this game." Quarrelling with Devyani, she says:

> A clever girl. . . . This game of chess is started only by you when you made me your slave, then your father and my mother and father also joined it. When you married Yayati, he joined too. Swaranlata joined as your loving maid and the people standing outside joined too. Now Yuvraj and his wife are going to join it. They too have to act as mohras in this game. (13)

This is how all the characters in *Yayati* are a party to the game of chess.

Symbolizing the inner alienation of Muhammad the game of chess in *Tughlaq* also stands for the complexity of the emperor as a person. For him, life is like a chess board where one's only aim is to win. His love for chess suggests his intricacies in relation to others. In scene II Muhammad tells Barani that he has invited Shihabudin, the prince of Shampanshahr because the Amirs there don't like his father and inviting his son would be a nice friendly gesture. When Barani questions this gesture saying "What's all this?" Muhammad answers, "Forgive me if I let you down Barani, but I must play this game on my own way" (160). Caught in his deft move, Imam-ud-Din too pleads, "Don't play any more games with me" (166). Despite Muhammad's verbal confession that "there is no time for games," he never stops playing it to the end. In his view, all the important persons around him are chess players. Barani, who is a historian, is only interested in playing chess "with the shadows of the dead." And Najib is a politician who wants "pawns of flood and flesh" (156). Similarly, when Aziz shouts at his counterpart not to call him by his name, the helpless Aazam retorts, "I'm fed up of these games." Christine Gomez rightly observes, "Chess symbolizes Tughlaq's game approach to life wherein he regards the other people as pawns to be manipulated for his own advantage."

As it demands isolation and aloofness from others the game of chess can also be equated with the rose-garden in *Tughlaq*. Both are Muhammad's love and can be taken as his desperate effort to get rid of his inner alienation. The rose garden which ends up as a "rubbish dump" is suggestive of the burial of Muhammad's dreams. He is found strolling alone at night in his garden. The heap of currency coins there symbolizes Muhammad's grave (a raised place) which he sees with his own eyes. Christine Gomez calls the Rose Garden an objective correlative: "The rose-garden which becomes a rubbish dump is a perfect objective correlative of Tughlaq's idealistic aspirations meeting with defeat. . . . It becomes an image of the absurd, the unbridgeable gulf between man's expectations of orderliness and the chaos and irrationality which confront him in the universe."

After the game of chess the next symbol of alienation in *Yayati* is the 'well.' Yayati meets Devyani for the first time when she has fallen into a well and is crying out for help. The 'well' symbolizes her suffering after she is isolated from her friend Sharmishtha. Trying to help her, Yayati metaphorically throws himself into the well. When he is cursed by Devyani's father, he actually feels like falling into a well. When Sharmishtha suggests to him to be at peace, he cries out; "Peace. . . . Peace, this peace . . . it is like falling into a bottomless well" (49).

There are empty courtyards, locked houses and deserted temples working as symbols in Karnad's plays. Rani in *Nagamandala* is locked in a house with a courtyard which has an anthill in it. The locked door stands for the constraints her husband has imposed on her feelings. Naga's entry into her room through a hole without touching the social lock put by Appanna is quite symbolic. Naga meets Rani keeping the 'lock' intact, i.e., without endangering her social image as a wife. Then the temples in *Hayavadana* and *Nagamandala* wear a deserted look. Here the candles assemble at night when the people fall asleep. The fort in *Tughlaq* built in Daulatabad, especially seen at night, becomes the symbol of a puzzle the emperor is embroiled in after leaving Delhi. The young guard describes the fort as a "magnificent thing" which no army could occupy. The fort, like the self of Muhammad and his rule, has "strange and frightening" passages within it. The guard rightly says, "If it ever falls it will crumble from the inside" (192). The description of the fort by the guard turns into a fantastic image of the rule of the emperor. The guard says that the road coming to the fort appears like a "thin snake" and the fort is like a "rising anthill." The old sentry holds, "Yes, it is a long passage, a big passage, coiled like an enormous hollow python inside the belly of the fort. And they shall be far happier when that python breaks out and swallows everything in sight—every man, woman, child and beast" (193). Here, Tughlaq is associated with a snake or python and his fort is the anthill; both are so inimical to the life of the common people.

The imagery of poison, death and destruction gets more pronounced when we find Karnad's characters frequently indulging in murder and violence. His plots are marked by bloodshed, famine, drought, starvation, poverty, flood and fire etc.

In *Tale-Danda* "the poor souls are tracked for weeks in search of food and shelter" (59). The drought "grips the land" in *The Fire and the Rain.* Then socio-religious affairs get vitiated through deceptions and murders. All the main characters seem to be affected by violence and death. If in *Yayati*, Chitralekha commits suicide by consuming poison, in *Tughlaq* murder and violence mark the main and the sub-plot. *Hayavadana* presents two friends stabbing each other on the stage followed by Padmini ending her own life. The cult of violence continues in *Tale-Danda* where the Sharanas' killings are followed by Bijjala and Jagadeva's death. *The Fire and the Rain* too shows the murder of Yavakri, Raibhya and the hunter girl.

Whereas the presence of deities, temples, mosques creates the milieu and speaks of the religious temper of the Indians in Girish Karnad, the orthodoxy of the socio-religious organization is suggested through trial by the village-courts. Rani in *Nagamandala* has to appear before the village court that asks her to undergo the purity-ordeal. In The *Fire and the Rain* too the social dictates are symbolized by the Elders of Nittilai's tribe. Before marrying the girl of their tribe every young man has to appear before them and get their nod. But in both the cases, the village-elders fail to know the reality and do justice to the claimants. Instead, they become a mockery of justice and truth.

The symbols used for love and sex are mostly traditional taken from Hindu mythology. The snake in *Nagamandala* can be viewed as a phallic symbol. It is through the king cobra that Rani meets her sexual urge and gets pregnant as a result. The snake or the cobra, is the symbol of sexuality. It is associated with "sexuality because of its phallic shape."[8] Sex is always viewed as poisonous by the society but it is pleasing to the individual. The cobra too is viewed poisonous by everyone except Rani. In Hindu mythology, a snake or Naga is awarded specific importance as the symbol of creation or procreation:

> In Hinduism, snakes are held to be both malevolent and benevolent creatures. . . . As symbols of dark and unknown recesses of the underground they are associated with creation and procreation, propagation and plentitude. The word 'Naga' itself results from double negatives (Na+aga) and refers to that which is 'not immobile' or 'which moves.' It carries with it association of all which teems, the ever flowing, indiscriminate abundance of nature, at one moment savage, at another moment serene. . . . To one who pleases them the prayers will be answered for fertility, petitions will be honoured for same deliveries.[9]

At the end of the play Rani permits the cobra to enter into her hair. Here, it becomes the phallic symbol and Rani's hair stand for the female sexual organ. As she says: "This hair is the symbol of my wedded bliss." (64).

Like the cobra the arrow becomes the phallic symbol in *The Fire and the Rain*. The sex-starved Vishakha wants to be killed by the arrow of her husband. She asks him to "pierce her" with the arrow before leaving her alone. In *Hayavadana*, Padmini's description of the moving bullock cart driven by Kapila has strong sexual overtones. The description of the journey by the cart when Kapila is driving it and Padmini is the rider becomes an allegory of the sexual act. Here the cart driven by the oxen stands for the Phallus, the bull for the male virility and the road the female sexual organ. Addressing Kapila, Padmini says, "The cart . . . the oxen seem to know exactly where to go—you drove it so gently" (95). But about Devadatta she says, "Devadatta took me in the cart—that was soon after our marriage. . . . So we started—only two of us, me and Devadatta driving against my advice. . . . And we didn't even cross the city gates. The oxen took everything except the road" (96). Then Kapila's description of the Fortunate Lady's flower is also suggestive of the female sexual organ, "The yellow on the petal . . . here-that thin saffron line like the parting of your hair—then . . . here near the stem a row of black dots" (9). Padmini calls it good for a simile. She is also called "Lotus," which apart from representing the beauty, also stands for the female generative organ. The Linga or the sacred Phallus in Hindu mythology is also depicted as resting on or surrounded by lotus petals symbolizing the unity between the male and the female as the secret of life in the universe. Then, 'bathing in a river' in *Hayavadana* stands for physical union. During conversation in the forest, Padmini reminds Kapila of the old relationship between their bodies by using the image of bathing in the river. She says, "Your body bathed in a river, swam and danced with it." Bhagavata rightly adds that the "river has no fear of memories," and the female chorus sings, "The river only feels the pull of the waterfall." In *Yayati* too, Sharmishtha and Devyani, have a bath in a river which was for the former an ecstatic experience of love.

As in the morality plays, the names of the characters in Karnad's plays also stand for their roles. In *Nagamandala*, Rani, meaning 'a queen' becomes the representative of all the middle class women living in a joint family in the patriarchal society. That is why "Her name . . . doesn't matter" (27), says the Story. Appanna also means 'everyone,' so he too is the representative of everyman in the male-dominated society. About Rani and the double role of Appanna, Pranav Joshipura holds that Rani in *Nagamandala* can be taken as a metaphor for the situation of a young girl in the bosom of a joint family where she sees her husband in two unconnected roles—as a stranger during the day and as a lover at night. The empty house Rani is locked in could be the family she is married into.

Then the characters in the sub-plot have also suggestive names. Kurudavva means 'blind' and her son Kappanna means the 'dark' one. So the 'dark' and the 'blind' together suggest the blindness of Rani in the dark of the night when Naga visits her bedroom.

Similarly in *Hayavadana* the names of the characters are true to their selves. Devadatta is the son of a Brahmin and like a Deva—a god—he is knowledgeable. Kapila, meaning 'iron,' has an iron-like body and Padmini meaning 'lotus' is beautiful like a flower. Her name becomes symbolic when we see that the lotus is rooted in the earth and with the flower turned skyward symbolizes "the fundamental nature (prakriti) of the human body. It is torn between the downward (tamasic) earth the upward (satvic) heavens, itself being impressionable (rajasic)." Thus her character and role are true to her name. Even Ganesha's head and a rat under it have symbolic significance. Ganesha has a head of an elephant forging ahead through all obstacles in the jungle. The rat, too, overcomes different obstacles in the fields and jungles. So, Ganesha with a rat stands for removing the obstacles. Its broken tusk and awkward belly symbolize the inherent idea of incompleteness and absurdity in human life. *Hayavadana* too with the head of an animal and body of a human being symbolizes the modern man: he is better than an animal but less than a perfect human being. G.H. Nayak also finds the symbolic importance of this semi-human being: "In *Hayavadana* an attempt is made among other things to symbolize ever so slightly the predicament of contemporary India as well as its future. The strange horse Hayavadana appears at the very beginning of the play almost as an average Indian citizen. Once this association draws upon us many other particulars in the play including the Kapila-Devadatta episode take on specific connotations relevant to the wider Indian context."[10]

The forests, jungles and gardens, apart from giving a folk-touch to Karnad's plays, serve as a symbol of self-searching after disenchantment with life. In *Yayati*, the king leaves for the forest after being disappointed. The forest life of renunciation and search is suggested to him by his maid, turned into a queen, when none of his subjects come forward to make a sacrifice. But Yayati rejects this offer. Finally, when he is challenged by his daughter-in-law, he himself prefers to quit for the forest life. Similarly the rose-garden apart from serving as a symbol of the daydreams of Muhammad, serves also as a symbol of search. After the total failure of his innovations with regard to the change of capital and new currency, he is seen roaming at night in the rose garden.

Like Yayati, Kapila in *Hayavadana* also leaves for the forest life after being disappointed by the Rishi's decision against him. The realization, that neither Devadatta nor Kapila belong to him, is very disappointing for him. Finding no meaning in human relationships, he prefers life in a forest. His journey to the forest is for the self-search as he has miserably failed to understand human relations. The *Fire and the Rain* has Yavakri who goes to the forests for higher knowledge, though this search is not human but spiritual.

Animals, birds and insects also figure in all the plays of Girish Karnad. Characters are compared with birds and animals. Yayati compares Sharmishtha with an "eagle," for her feeling of jealousy and hatred. Similarly, Muhammad's stepmother calls him a "pompous ass" and says that she doesn't wish his fate even "on a dog." Even the road to Daulatabad looks to him like "a snake" and the old man calls it the "eagle's nest" (192). If the passage in the fort is "like a python," the palace is "full of flies." The people around him appear to Muhammad as "vultures." After ordering the death of his mother, he feels himself as a "pig" rolling in the gory mud. In *Hayavadana* the temples of Rudra including Padmini's house are full of bats, snakes and all sorts of poisonous insects. One of the Dolls complains that in Padmini's house "a mouse rubbed its feet and a cockroach at its eyes" (115). In *Nagamandala*, Rani daydreams being carried away by an "eagle" standing for her imaginary flight. She also dreams of a "whale" coming to her on a rainy day. Then she finds a "stag" at her door saying that it is not a stag but "a prince" of her dreams. If Rani is like a "caged bird," Appanna is like a "wild beast" or "a reptile." He brings suffering to Rani who endures it without protest like a "pig, the whale and the eagle" (45). Similarly, the jungle wherein Yavakri carried on her penance, is full of flies, giants, ants, beetles, leeches, viper and mosquitoes as is the temple of Rudra in

Hayavadana. Thus we find life in Karnad's plays as marked by the imagery of insects and animals hinting at the absurdity of life.

The image of shifting from one form to another or from one place to another marks almost every play of Karnad. In *Yayati* this shift is witnessed through Yayati's change into his son's youth and son's youth and return to his old self. In *Tughlaq* this shift is physically made by Muhammad by changing his capital from Delhi to Daulatabad and back again. Then Padmini in *Hayavadana* goes from Devadatta to Kapila and back to her husband. *Nagamandal*a too has this shift in the double role of Appanna. Rani has to move from Appanna at night to Appanna during the day. In *Tale-Danda* the king likes and dislikes the Sharanas and their ideology shifting from one stand to the other. This sort of shift symbolizes the inherent duality in the mind of the playwright.

Use of Language

As regards the language used by Karnad, it is very fluent, natural and flawless. It reveals the socio-economic status of the characters and suits their roles so well. Muhammad's language shows his wide learning, his complex personality and his imperial background. His visions are those of a philosopher: "You are asking me to make myself complete killing the Greeks in me and you propose to unify my people by denying the visions which led Zarathustra or the Buddha" (165). Then he refers to Sukrat, Aflatoon and Kuran as well. On the other hand, being a low-caste, the king in *Tale-Danda* uses rustic language. He calls himself "Kalachuriya," "Rough hewn" and "blunt." His son for him is a "son of a whore," "eunuch" hiding "between his mother's legs" etc. However, the language used by Basavanna is that of a saint and philosopher:

> I don't have in me
> bhakti enough
> to equal a sixth
> of a mustard seed

I'm an ekka, a swallow-wort
among mangoes.
How can I shamelessly
Call myself a devotee? (23)

The playwright is adept in the use of poetic and imaginative language. The cobra's expressions suit his romantic nature so well. He addresses Rani as, "Rani! My queen! The fragrance of my nights! The blossom of my dreams" (61).

Interestingly, Karnad's stern faith in the basic human passions and his bitter attitude towards the social ills results in pointed dialogues that serve serious and comic purposes:

Nittilai: Do you know why father called the elders in such haste? He always says 'These high caste men are glad enough to bed out women but not to wed them.'
Arvasu: All right. Now I shall wed you so you can . . .
Nittilai: (*Screams*) Shut up! (*They all laugh*) (8)

Idioms and phrases mark Karnad's dramatic verve adding to the lucidity and flexibility of expression. Moreover, native words and expressions are used freely by him. If *Tughlaq* is full of Indian and Arabic words, such as 'Sultan,' 'Jazia,' 'Durbar-I-khas' and 'Dhobi'; the other plays also have words like 'Punya,' 'Sanjeevani,' 'Faqir,' 'Rishi,' 'Sari,' 'Sati,' 'Yajna' etc. Even the characters from Indian mythology, like Naga, Kali, Ganesha, Brahman Rakshasa inhabit his dramatic universe. Some Indian expressions are literally translated into chaste English: "In her house, the very floor is swept by the goddess of wealth. In Devadatta's house, they've the goddess of learning for a maid" (90). There are so many examples of the sort.

Thus we see that Girish Karnad attempts a wonderful blend of devices from the traditional Indian and modern western theatres. His experiment with the folk devices exercises a lot of appeal upon the modern sensibility. As a result, his plays are eminently theatrical for the audience along with their past significance and present meaning they reflect for the readers.

NOTES

1. Girish Karnad spoke at 'Meet the Author Programme' organized by the Sahitya Akademi and the India International Centre, on 16 November, 1988. The same lecture was later published under the title "Acrobating between the Traditional and the Modern."
2. Vardhapande, "The Sutradhar," *Tradition of Indian Theatre*, (Delhi: Abhinav, 1979), p. 93.
3. "Girish Karnad: An Interview with Kirtinath Kurtkoti," *Contemporary Indian Theatre: Interview with Playwrights and Directors*, p. 82-83.
4. M.S. Varadpande, "Dancing Dolls," *Invitation to Indian Theatre* (New Delhi: Arnold, 1978), p.63.
5. Reeta Sondhi, "*Hayavadana*: A Continuing Search," *Enact*, 205-6, Jan.-Feb. 1984.
6. "Girish Karnad: An Interview with Kirtinath Kurtkoti," p. 82.
7. M.L. Varadpande, p.41.
8. *The Encyclopedia of World Mythology* (Herrgkorg: Mandaine, 1979), p. 214.
9. H. Daniel Smith and M. Narsimachary, *Handbook of Hindu Goddesses, Gods and Saints* (Delhi: Sandeep, 1991), p.237.
10. G.H. Nayak, "Kannada," *Indian Literature since Independence*, ed. K.R. Srinivasa Iyengar (Madras: Sahitya Akademi, 1987) p. 105.

The Oedipus Complex in Counterpoint: A Comparative Study of Girish Karnad's *Yayati* and Sant Singh Sekhon's *Fate*

Girish Karnad and Sant Singh Sekhon are modern Indian playwrights writing in their respective regional languages. Girish Karnad is an actor, director of theatre and film and above all an innovative playwright of post-Independence India. Originally written in Kannada, most of his plays have been translated into English. Sant Singh Sekhon (1908-1997), on the other hand, was a renowned Punjabi playwright. Though he started his literary career as a poet in English yet his plays remained untranslated during his lifetime. (Now Sahitya Akademi, New Delhi, has come out with English translation of his plays on Sikh History). Though belonging to different regions and having specificities of their own, both the playwrights have much in common. Karnad's plays are marked mainly by the existentialist thought of Jean-Paul Sartre and Albert Camus, and Sekhon's vision is coloured by the Marxian ideology. He views everything from the historical and dialectical angle. As a result a critique termed by him as *Nirvachin* (new and renewed interpretation) becomes the hallmark of his plots. But one thing that unites the two playwrights is their fondness for tradition. They derive their stories from their own culture and history and view them in the light of modern sensibility. So, the mythical and historical events become vehicles for modern thinking under the impact of western ideologies and systems of knowledge. As an example, a Freudian overtone is the distinguishing mark of both the plays taken for study in this paper. A discussion of Karnad's *Yayati*[1] in counterpoint with Sant Singh Sekhon's one act play *Fate*[2] seems deeply relevant in this regard. It becomes important in the light of what Raymond Williams, one of the greatest litterateur thinkers of the 20th century, upheld in the following words:

> Greek tragic action was not rooted in individual, or in individual psychology in any of our senses. It was rooted in history, and not a human history alone. Its thrust came not from the personality of individual but from a man's inheritance and relationships.[3]

The Oedipus tale as it occurs in the Greek mythology has historical and cultural elements inherent in it. The plight of Oedipus cannot be understood by cutting it off from the primitive times, its culture and ethos. The prophecy of the oracle, the birth of Oedipus, killing of the King Laius, Oedipus's marriage with his own mother—all happen in a pre-determined way. The more Oedipus runs away from his ordained fate, the more he gets close to his tragic end. Learning at the end that he has killed none other than his own father and the queen he has got with the kingdom is his own mother, Oedipus blinds himself and the queen commits suicide. He takes full responsibility for what destiny does to him. In this way his complex, with which his name gets inextricably entangled, stands for the impulse to be human, to catch destiny by the forelock and not be subsumed by the blind forces of nature. In his pursuit to know himself he undoes himself. Thus in this tale, past and future are closely knit together; Oedipus's present cannot be separated either from his past or his future.

But in Sigmund Freud's psychoanalysis, the concept of the Oedipus complex has its face turned to the past. For the individual's trouble in the present and future it holds the past, even the pre-natal one, fully responsible. The son starts loving his mother from his very childhood, holds Freud. Rather, the mother is the first object of erotic attachment for the male child. So, to Freud the Oedipus complex simply implies an incestuous attachment of the son to his mother and the resultant feeling of hatred for the father because, for the child he is an intruder. Commenting on this triangular relationship, Calvin S. Hall observes: "Prior to the emergence of the phallic period, a boy loves his mother and identifies with his father; when the sexual urge increases the boy's love for his mother becomes more incestuous and as a result he becomes jealous of his rival, the father. This tale of affair in which the boy causes exclusive sexual possession of his mother and feels antagonistic towards his father, is called the Oedipus Complex."[4]

From this perspective we see that the relationship between the father and the son in Girish Karnad's play is Freudian whereas in Sant Singh Sekhon's play it takes after its mythical version overloaded with historical and cultural connotations.

In Sekhon's *Fate* the relationship between Maan Singh, the ruler of Gangapur, and his son Vijay Singh, the Crown Prince, seems to border on the Oedipus complex. Vijay Singh loves Rajeshwari, the queen of Bhanpur, who, having escaped the Sultan's siege, takes refuge in the palace of Maharana Maan Singh. The Maharana has a great infatuation for her young daughter but his own son happens to fall in love with the queen. This triangle upsets the Maharana and the young prince a lot. In order to avenge themselves on each other, both tend to sabotage each other's plan.

As the play opens, Vijay Singh, obsessed with his infatuation for Brajeshwari, desperately urges Vishwanath, the minister, to intervene and persuade the king not to persist in this path. He calls this relationship a 'scandal', albeit 'revolting' because the girl is not even "sixteen years old." In no way does she make a match for his father who is three times her age. For him it is an enormity that his "father over fifty years old, should lust for a girl of sixteen" (126). The idea that he seems to stress is the huge gap between the two, as Brajeshwari is of the age of the king's granddaughter. Terming it "utterly damnable," he urges the minister to "ponder over" it.

The issue of love and sexuality in the play gets further crucial when Vishwanath also admits that beauty bewitches the king and it is his "fate." "He is helpless. After every five years, the grand passion wakes up in him. Such is the fate of his passion. How long it is since he married before the last time? About ten years, on my count" (128). In fact falling in love has become a "habit" with him, holds he. At this, Vijay Singh pledges to change the rhythm of his father's passion. But why he is so much averse to the king's relationship with Brajeshwari, and why the king is so averse to the relationship between Vijay Singh and Rajeshwari is an enigma that gets further intractable when the Minister enquires of Vijay Singh the reason why he opposes the king, "Is it that your stepmother is so young or . . . Brajeshwari is a mere girl." At this Vijay Singh reveals his true intention saying, "I don't relish his leaving behind a legacy of wretched stepmothers for me. And I am deeply hurt to think that an innocent girl like Brajeshwari is being made a victim of his demonic passion" (128). However, he fails to explicate the reason behind his own attachment with the mother of the princess. Ironically, he regards Brajeshwari as his younger sister, "rather a daughter." The reason he offers in support of his argument is that she does not look "even sixteen." At no cost is he ready to see her fall victim to the sexual desire of his father.

He proclaims that he would rather like her being "slaughtered like a lamb" at the altar of the goddess Kali. The contradiction in his argument and the reason behind his rivalry with his father is pointed out by the minister who holds, "Prince this is not a good omen. You are twenty two and Brajeshwari is sixteen. Your feeling also seems unusual" (128). It would have been remarkable, says he, if his father had fallen in love with Rani Rajeshwari. But the playwright makes the position of the Prince untenable when he says, "No, not even that. What need has my father to fall in love with a woman" and the minister comments, "It is not a matter of one's needs. For that matter, nobody needs fall in love" (128).

The feminine side of sexuality is awarded due representation by the playwright. An interesting aspect of the situation is that Rajeshwari and Brajeshwari are mother and daughter and the persons they love also happen to be father and son in relationship. The mother loves the son and the daughter loves his father. The point to take notice is that both are in search of a male figure and unconsciously they select the person who suits their emotional needs the most. Rajeshwari finds it in Vijay Singh who is younger and energetic and Brajeshwari in the old king who is powerful. In the place of youth she compromises on power. Perhaps, her fiancé's helplessness in the battlefield that he displayed by fleeing from Bhanpur induces her to love the king. The intensity of passion burdened with the sexual jealousy of the two women can be better understood from the "stringent talk" between Rajeshwari and Vishwanath as the latter says, "No, Rana Rawindra's cowardice is not the reason of her being entangled with the king." The real cause, says he, lies in "jealousy":

> But it is not a child's play to disappoint one as beautiful and dignified as Brajeshwari. You have seen the result of disappointment with Rana Rawindra. Can't we bring the prince round to transfer his love to Brajeshwari? . . . And I know, however strongly the Maharana may feel about it, he will not be his son's rival. (132)

But she is not at all ready to accept this solution. Asked to help her daughter, as mothers as a rule help their daughters in alleviating their anguish, she flatly refuses: "I for one can't do so" (132). When suggested to quench her "rage," her "jealousy," she retorts:

> Why should she be jealous, why should she resent? (*Breaking into sobs)* Should she be jealous of me? . . . The prince can't give her that kind of love as he regards her as a daughter. Had I known my own daughter would get into rivalry with me, I would never have tried to escape from Jauhar. Now she is offended with me and out of jealousy she is bent on surrendering her youth to that old scoundrel. O God! How harsh is your justice. (133)

The dialogue between Rajeshwari and Vishwanath further reveals the intricate situation both have got into:

> Rajeshwari: But why does the Maharana thus exploit my daughter's jealousy?
>
> Vishwanath: My master does not know that Brajeshwari is doing it all out of jealousy.

> Rajeshwar: Why not? He knows it for certain.
> Vishwanath: It is possible he may himself also be doing all this out of a pique. My master thinks of your highness the same as you think of him (133)

Irony of the situation is that she loves the prince who is younger to her in age but she can't imagine her daughter loving the old king: "Never, never will I concede that Brajeshwari loves the Maharana." Her jealousy comes to the fore when she screams, "If he marries her I know how to avenge myself" (135). To further prove the point it is appropriate to quote Sekhon: "The feeling of jealousy between the mother and the daughter is very powerful in *Fate,* this killing-jealousy is the fate."

The feeling of sexual jealousy between the father and the son no more remains a secret when the Prince calls his father a "rogue" and the Maharana calls him a "bastard," a "fool" and Rajeshwari "a whore." The father warns him: "And I will not let you sniff at the air that flows touching Brajeshwari's garments!" Physically assaulted, the son also pounces on the father, "You old bull! This is the reward for violating so many virgins" (*He drives the sword into Maharana's chest).* Both fall down dead on the ground and Brajeshwari takes poison. Thus completes the circle of the Oedipal relationship.

But the idea of sexuality gets a different meaning in Sekhon when he criticizes the Maharana for whom woman and love is the only and ultimate purpose of life. He forgets his duties as a king and seeks solace in gratification of his sexual urge. Vishwanath repeatedly warns him to "extinguish his passion" and be wary about the fact that "women are the instruments of fate." But to the Maharana's mind, "love is stronger than fate." Here Sekhon seems to be apprehensive of the consequences of this tragic obsession of the king. He is ready to pay "too high a price . . . for love." Brajeshwari loves him and feels he is very brave. Ironically, the prince regards Brajeshwari his daughter as she is "hardly sixteen" but the Maharana regards her the most suitable match because she is "over eighteen" in his eyes. The playwright appears to make Vishwanath his spokesman when the latter asks the king to "keep women at arm's length" and makes him realize that "love is the second name of fate. For the sake of the kingdom and its people whose guardian God has appointed Your Highness, the sacrifice should be made" (137). To this suggestion his answer is: "Love is stronger than Fate." And "if this is fate I do not bother at all," holds he. This is how he heads towards his ruinous end and Vishwanath remains only a spectator to the tragedy that is imminent. The encounter that follows between the father and the son is typically Freudian in nature. Admitting the psychological insight displayed by the playwright, Balwant Gargi observes, "I like this play very much—jealousy between the mother and the daughter, inner hatred in the relationship of the father and son, the intense love of both for the mismatched women is the outcome of a deep mental and psychological insight (on the part of the playwright)."

Such scenes where the father and the son are face to face blaming each other using language laden with sexual imagery are very common in Girish Karnad. His *Yayati* is the representative play in this respect. The relationship between Yayati and Puru also appears to border on the Oedipus complex. If the Maharaja in Sekhon's *Fate* loves a girl who is a more suitable match for his son, Karnad's Yayati, the king, seduces his attendant in the absence of his wife, that too on the bed where his own newly wedded son and his wife had to consummate their marriage. When he is cursed for his act with old age, his son willingly offers himself to take the curse on his head and as a result becomes older than his father. Significantly, he takes the place of his father in relation to his own mother.

Even as a child Puru has harboured the feeling of excessive attachment to his mother and that of resentment and hatred against his father. When he was away from his mother he always missed her. He admits that her mother's memories always haunted him.

He would miss even the room where he used to be with his mother: "my dear room! The room of a few moment of joy in life" (42). He always dreams of his mother. Such questions as, "Who was she? What was she like?" (44) defy any resolution by him. In all respects he hints at his attraction for his mother but Yayati fails to understand it. Puru laments that his father never had time to know his inner feelings. To give vent to his feelings of love for his mother, "he was always restless" (41). Puru does not hesitate to tell Yayati that his existence for him is only in terms of his love for his mother. Thus his decision to accept the old age of his father seems to be an attempt towards satisfying the desire of his unconscious mind. "Who was she? What was she like?" (42), is the question he always poses to his father. He is not reluctant to confess that he has spent his childhood for "that one face"; when Yayati does not give any satisfactory answer, he literally starts crying. Puru's hatred for Yayati is not a secret either. As for Freud the father is always an obstacle between the son and his mother; Puru's hatred for his father is not without meaning. Yayati too is aware of this hostility when he confesses, "Whenever we talk to each other, there erupts a quarrel. Why is it so? This I have not been able to know so far" and Puru "vomits fire" (49) seeing him.

The relationship between Yayati and Sharmishtha is that of a king and his pretty attendant. Though she has dismissed her right to be the equal of Devyani—her old friend and the present queen of the king—by meekly accepting her new role as an attendant in the king's palace, yet she has not outrightly rejected her inner feminine self. She says that she "had once that scent of youth; I would die for the smell of land that is caused by the first sprinkle of the rain, I would stroll in trees and plants to see a spider weaving a shiny net in the light of the sun" (21). It shows the burning desire in her to be one with her opposite sex. Narrating the tale of her sexual frustration and finding no outlet for her suppressed desires she attempts to take poison. But Yayati would not let her die. Like the Maharana in *Fate,* Yayati's attraction for the female sex transcends all social barriers and he shares the bed with Sharmishtha, his attendant. As she attempts to take poison he checks her holding her by the right hand. Reminded of the meaning of holding the hand of a stranger woman, he withdraws it at once and he orders his attendant to leave. He commands, "Don't let anybody enter unless I myself call" and "sits by her on the same bed" (26-27). In the next scene he is found smiling and Sharmishtha's hair is "spread over her shoulders." Covering her head with her sari, she sits near him Significantly, this meeting elevates her from an attendant to a queen. Yayati too feels young again as he tells Devyani, "I was feeling old. Sharmishtha has enthused me, returned my youth to me. I cannot leave her" (35).

As the price of the sexual jealousy between the father and the son is paid by Rajeshwari in *Fate,* in *Yayati* the victim of the jealousy is Puru's wife—Chitralekha. She also takes poison like Rajeshwari and kills herself. Chitralekha too is conscious and assertive about herself. She becomes the spokesperson of her husband, Puru. She accuses the king of exchanging his old age with her husband's youth. She pledges not to see her husband in Anantpur until he regains his youth. She lashes out at her father-in-law, 'You are the man to push him [Puru] near funeral . . . and you are advising me without knowing my grief" (73-74). She expresses her inability to hide her real self under the 'mask' of thoughts which he is wearing. As he promises her that he will give the borrowed youth back after fulfilling his aim, she questions him, "Can you imagine what will be his age by the time you complete your aim. . . . I got this youth just for fifteen days before: What are you talking of your six year?" (75) She values her present far more than the future of his kingdom and challenges him to accept the reality relating to the youth of her husband: "You snatched away youth from my husband. It is logical that you accept everything concerning it" (77). When she realizes that nothing is going to help her she takes poison like Rajeshwari in Sekhon's *Fate.*

Thus we find that Oedipus complex seems to be the meeting ground between Girish Karnad and Sant Singh Sekhon, notwithstanding the fact that sexuality has been viewed differently by the two playwrights. Sekhon in his *Fate* is critical of the Maharana and his son who are bent on crossing all limits to show each other down in love for women. For them woman is the only issue of dispute, and, for their people and the state they have no vision. From this angle the title of the one act play, *Fate,* is important because for the king and his son woman becomes fate and fate becomes woman. In Girish Karnad the idea of Oedipus complex operates in a mythical story but his treatment is different. He employs the oedipal pattern of relationship as such and weaves it in the Freudian sense. But the visions of both the playwrights are valuable in their own way—as together they constitute an important aspect of modern Indian drama. They may belong to two different languages but they certainly are a part of an important stream of Indian drama.

NOTES

1 Girish Karnad, *Yayati* (New Delhi: Saraswati Press, 1964). All subsequent translated textual references to the next are from this Hindi edition.

2 Sant Singh Sekhon, *Fate,* trans. Tejwant S. Gill, *Indian Literature,* 207, Jan 2002, 126-38.

3 Raymond Williams, "From Hero to Victim" *Modern Tragedy* (London: Chatto & Windus, 1969), pp. 87-88.

4 Calvin S. Hall, *A Primer of Freudian Psychology* (New York: The New American's Press, 1957), p. 110.

5 Balwant Gargi, "College Da Vice Chancellor," *Sharbat Dian Ghuttan* (Slipping Sweet Drink) (New Delhi, Navyug, 1996), p. 203.

6 *Ibid.*, p. 217.

7 *Ibid.*, p. 21.